T0356483

The Bread Machine Book

COLOR

The Bread Machine Book

75 Unforgettable, Unfussy Recipes
for Every Baker

Lukas Volger
Photographs by Trevor Baca

TEN SPEED PRESS
California | New York

Contents

This Old Thing?

I think I was nine or ten years old when my family got a bread machine. This was the early '90s, and at the time they were a signifier of modernity, easy domestic prowess, and middle-class suburban comfort, steadily appearing in the kitchens of many of my mom's friends. But I cared little about what they represented. Instead, I was enamored of the squishy, doughy loaves that emerged from them.

My brother and I would slather our slices with Country Crock margarine while they were still emanating steam, and then we'd cram them into our mouths, compressing a whole piece of bread into a single, Play-Doh–like ball. We thought it was the most ideal texture imaginable: gummy, gooey, good. All the loaves I made at that time came from packaged bread mixes, but it was still such a marvel. Homemade bread by the press of a button? A button that I pressed? Incredible!

My first bread machine affair didn't last all that long, though. A year or so later, its mixing paddle got baked into a loaf and was accidentally tossed into the garbage with a stale heel, a familiar fate for fellow (and former) bread machine owners. Soon enough, the appliance seemed like a passing fad anyway.

But I can mark that period as an awakening, and the bread machine as a gateway to a lifelong passion. In a few years, I'd be working summers at Stone Mill Bread Company in Boise, Idaho, where in addition to tending the cash register and bagging sticky cinnamon-swirl bread, I was scooping flour from 32-gallon trash cans set on dollies, reaching all the way to my armpits into the funky depths of a bucket of sourdough starter to feed and mix it by hand, and portioning out dough with a bench scraper. I was learning, hands-on, about the levers of time, temperature, and yeast that miraculously transform wet flour into delicious bread.

I went on to cook in restaurant kitchens while attending college in New York, which is where I continue to live, and ultimately built a career as a cookbook author. And while my focus eventually shifted from baking to vegetable-centric savory cooking, my sourdough starter was almost always bubbling away in my fridge. From my Brooklyn studio apartment, I'd go through long stretches of turning out tangy, crusty, Tartine-style loaves every few days, giving them away to anyone who'd take them. New York City is a bread lover's paradise—with excellent bakeries scattered liberally across the five boroughs—but the unique satisfaction of tearing into a fresh, homemade loaf has never once lost its grip on me.

So, when the opportunity came up several years ago to test out a half-dozen bread machines for a freelance project, I was skeptical. I'd long outgrown that retro appliance, and cultivated an appreciation for high-hydration sourdough country loaves with wide-open crumbs and thick, crackly crusts. I mean, I had a bread *practice.* What on earth did I need this machine for?

A lot, I soon found out. While bread machines aren't perfect (what appliance is?), I discovered that they really excel at mixing, kneading, and proofing dough. Doing these tasks by hand can be a pleasure, sure, but it's equally pleasurable to have the mess contained, the dough proofed to perfection, and for the whole process to require little to no attention or intervention.

Nowadays, I've got the toasty aroma of my 100% whole wheat loaf wafting from the kitchen at least twice a week. Homemade hamburger buns are a pretty reasonable thing to whip up on short notice to bring to a friend's BBQ.

And I've discovered the thrill of homemade bagels on a lazy Saturday—why had I denied myself for so long? Sure, the appliance has some shortcomings (how about a paddle-shaped gash in the bottom of your bread, or the comically tall, R2-D2–shaped loaves that some models yield?), but as you'll discover in the pages that follow, these quirks are easy to work with or overcome.

And while I was busy revisiting the bread machine, coming to regard it not as a replacement for a breadmaking practice but as a tool for enhancing and streamlining it, I learned that scores of bakers across the world had never lost any affection for theirs. They capitalized on its best features right away. Or they embraced the machine to adapt to lifestyle changes interfering with their breadmaking routines, such as when kneading and handling dough became difficult due to injuries or conditions that limited their mobility in the kitchen.

Others got into homemade bread during COVID stay-at-home orders, when sourdough starter became a staple of many home kitchens. With the flexibility to attend to the finicky schedule of homemade sourdough, these cooks came to appreciate the delicious ROI on home-baked bread. But with post-pandemic life reasserting its pre-pandemic demands, the bread machine presented itself as a helpful compromise—a way to keep fresh bread on hand without as much oversight.

And in 2023, Christina Morales of the *New York Times* reported that a new generation was taking to bread machines to cut down on grocery costs during inflation. Snagging inexpensive secondhand models online or at Goodwill stores, home cooks and TikTok influencers were using them to make better bread with ingredients of their choosing, at less than half the cost of what grocery stores were charging for the commercially made stuff. Morales's article noted a 20 percent surge in sales for bread machines that year.

So obviously I've only been catching up to the collective mood.

If you own any other bread books, you may have noticed that bread can inspire quite a passion for science and technique. There's a lot to know. But for me, an overload of detail can be overwhelming, so I've tried not to approach this book that way. It isn't written from the scientific or overly exacting point of view that distinguishes many bread cookbooks. As I see it, the bread machine was designed to make life easier, and my goal is to share recipes that channel its inherent ease.

In the next chapter I take more of a deep dive into the process, with helpful guidelines and tips to lead you on your journey. But know that this book is chiefly a celebration of, and perhaps an invitation to reconsider, a uniquely useful kitchen appliance, one that probably should never have gone out of fashion. My passion for cooking and baking started with a bread machine, and with this, I catalog a full-circle moment, taking me back to where it began.

1

Bread Machine 101

This book is a little different from other bread machine cookbooks. If you don't have time to read this entire chapter before you start baking, here are the two most important takeaways:

→ Gram measurements come before volume ones, because baking is quicker, tidier, and more precise when you use a digital scale.

→ Most recipes include two method options. The first, which uses a pre-programmed setting, is for a set-it-and-forget-it loaf that will turn out great but might not be *perfect*. The second includes opportunities to intervene, such as to shape your loaf by hand, slow down the fermentation, and/or to bake in your own oven, which allows you to exert more control and achieve more attractive results.

PROGRAMS
1. WHITE
2. FRENCH
3. WHOLE WHEAT
4. ULTRA-FAST
5. SWEET
6. GLUTEN FREE
7. ARTISAN DOUGH
8. DOUGH
9. JAM
10.PACKAGED MIX
11. CAKE
12. BAKE
PROG
COLOR
3:25
SIZE /
START
STOP

Pros and Cons of a Bread Machine

A bread machine is an incredibly useful tool that can make the habit of homemade bread a fully achievable reality. But like all appliances, there are certain things it's better at than others. The purpose of starting with pros and cons is to set your expectations, allow you to begin simmering up some possibilities, and set the tone for why I'm so obsessed with intervening to adapt the machine's functions for your own desired results.

Pros

→ **Hands-off:** Add your ingredients to the baking pan, snap it into place, press start, and you'll have a loaf of bread within a few hours.

→ **Good for gluten:** It's great at kneading dough and built for long kneading sessions.

→ **Powerful proofing:** You don't have to worry too much about finding a warm spot for your dough to rise—it has built-in conditions that help yeast flourish.

→ **Energy efficient:** There's no preheat necessary, it uses much less energy to bake than your oven, and produces a lot less wasted residual heat as well.

→ **Minimized mess:** From spurts of flour to splotchy work surfaces, it contains all the mess. And if you use a scale to measure your ingredients, there'll be hardly any dishes to clean!

Cons

→ **Moderate heat:** Its moderate heat (between 325° and 350°F) produces thin, usually pale crusts, rather than burnished, crackly, thick ones.

- → **Very fast to rise:** Fast proofing is good for a fast loaf, but not so great for flavor and the structure generated by longer, slower, cooler conditions, such as with sourdough bread.
- → **Uneven baking:** Depending on your model, the tops of breads don't always brown, and in some cases, bake unevenly.
- → **Wonky shapes:** You may end up with some misshapen loaves (though they'll hopefully still taste delicious) and there will most likely be paddle-shaped cavities in the base.
- → **One size fits all:** A bread machine imposes its own system on what has historically been a sensory process, so it can't adapt to variable conditions like humidity and temperature.

How a Bread Machine Works

While bread machine models vary from one to the next, across the category the mechanics are largely the same, featuring a few key parts:

- → A removable baking pan fitted with a rotating, removable paddle (or two)
- → A lidded compartment that the baking pan snaps into, connecting the kneading paddle to the machine's motor, where all the action takes place
- → A coiled heating element, which typically wraps around the lower part of the pan
- → An interface with baking presets and a display screen

TIMER
CANCEL
START

CANCEL
COURSE
CRUST CONTROL
TIME SETTING
START
TIMER
CYCLE
ZOJIRUSHI
BB-SSC10

Variables from one model to the next include:

- → The shape of the baked loaf—a tall, upright one, or a more traditional horizontal shape
- → The strength and durability of the machine's motor
- → The evenness of the heating element
- → The quality and range of presets
- → The number and types of kneading paddle—some models have two paddles, and some have paddles that fold down after kneading to minimize the hole in the base of the finished loaf

My Favorite Bread Machine

If you're shopping for a bread machine, start by asking, "How often will I use it?" If you expect to bake with it frequently, it's probably worth splurging on an upper quality model, such as the Zojirushi Virtuoso Plus. I've tested over a half dozen bread machines, and this is my favorite, and a top pick among product reviewers and other bread machine enthusiasts, too.

It produces traditionally shaped loaves; has a durable nonstick lining on the pan; includes two paddles instead of one, which mix and knead well; is built with a strong, long-lasting motor; and has top- and bottom-heating elements that are better for browning and baking the loaf evenly. And unlike most other models, its interface allows you to create custom programs to set the amount of time for kneading, proofing, and baking, so that you can easily isolate certain functions and use the machine for more than just set-it-and-forget-it loaves.

That said, all bread machines are useful for hands-free kneading and proofing dough—and if you like the bread your machine is producing, by all means: carry on! You'll find plenty of fun recipes here to broaden your repertoire.

Tips for Success

Add Ingredients in the Correct Order

In the eight different bread machines I've baked with, the order of ingredients is always the same: wet ingredients on the bottom, dry ones on top, and yeast last. This not only prevents the yeast from becoming activated too early should it come into contact with water if the machine has a resting period, but also better mixes dough, similar to how it's best to load up a blender with the wet, easy-to-blend stuff on the bottom. Your bread machine may be different, and if it is, please refer to your instruction manual and swap the order if needed. In this book, we add wet ingredients first, and dry on the top.

Please Use a Digital Scale

You'll see that gram measurements are shown before volume ones—for example, "130g" goes before "1 cup" for bread flour—and this is for two reasons. First, it's much more precise, especially with flour. One volume cup of flour can weigh anywhere between 120 and 150 grams depending on how you scoop it, spoon it, or pack it in, and such a range of variance really adds up when there are 3 to 4 cups of flour in a given loaf, drastically affecting the outcome.

Also, it's just so much easier—and eliminates most of the dirty dishes! Simply place your baking pan directly on the scale and weigh each ingredient in it straight out of its container, resetting (or "taring") the scale to zero between them. This allows you to use exactly as much flour as I would like you to. And I think you'll find it to be even more of a perk with sticky, messy ingredients like honey and molasses.

Spooned and Leveled Flour Measuring Method

If you're not using a digital scale to measure flour, use the "spooned and leveled" method: Spoon flour into your measuring cup without tapping it or packing it in, then use something flat, like the dull side of a table knife, to level off the top against the rim.

KING ARTHUR
BAKING COMPANY
UNBLEACHED
BREAD
FLOUR
WHEAT
ORGANIC SIFTED ALL-PURPOSE FLOUR
MAINE
GRAINS
zero
lb/kg

Don’t Be Afraid to Check the Dough

Just because a bread machine is meant to be a set-it-and-forget-it operation does not mean you can’t periodically pause the machine or peek in to check its progress. In fact, it’s a good idea to examine your dough every now and then. Here are a few points when it’s helpful to check, and even to intervene:

→ **While the dough is mixing:** You may notice that patches of dough or flour are stuck to the sides or corners of the pan. Pause the machine and use a flexible spatula to scrape them into the dough. This is also a good opportunity to evaluate the dough and decide if another tablespoon of flour or liquid is necessary, which can be important if you’re baking in very humid or dry conditions.

→ **During the first rise:** If I have the time, I like to briefly handle the dough once it’s kneaded to give it something of a “stretch and fold,” to evaluate its strength and progress. Just reach into the machine, gently pull on one end of the dough, and fold it over the center, and repeat on the opposite side.

→ **Shape after the final punch-down:** If you wish, you can pull the dough from the machine, remove the paddles, shape your loaf by hand, and return it to the machine. This improves the doming on the bread and creates a more attractive shape. Also, if you intend to bake the bread in a standard loaf pan in your home oven, this would be the time to take it out of the machine.

Use Room Temperature or Tepid Ingredients

Because bread machines generate heat during mixing and rising, they’re more likely to overproof a loaf than underproof it. So, to slow down proofing slightly and as a form of insurance, I start with room temperature or tepid liquids rather than warm ones.

Opportunities for Intervention

To Slow Down the Process and Develop Flavor Through Fermentation

Making bread is traditionally a very sensory process, utilizing time as an ingredient not only for giving dough the opportunity to inflate with gas and develop its trademark crumb, but to help build flavor, too. The bread machine skillfully automates this element, saving home cooks all the trouble. But depending on your schedule and desired outcomes, you may want to slow down the bread machine process. Here's when it's best to intervene.

→ **Right after kneading is complete:** Almost every preset bread machine cycle begins with kneading (some, like the Zojirushi, start with a resting period that allows the ingredients to all come to temperature). As soon as the dough is kneaded and before it starts its bulk fermentation in the machine (which will heat up the dough and fast-track its rise), stop the cycle and remove the dough. Transfer it to an airtight container (a 2-quart size works great) and move it to a cool spot or to the fridge. There, it will undergo its bulk rise more slowly. And if you wish to further slow its fermentation, you can reduce the yeast by half, too. This is a particularly useful step in sourdough loaves to build more pronounced, tangy flavors. But give it up to an hour to come back to room temperature once removing it from the fridge and before baking.

Removing the Paddles for Baking

One way to get rid of the unsightly paddle cavities from the bottom of a bread machine loaf is to simply remove the paddles after the final punch-down, which is when you'd shape the loaf if you choose to. But if you do this, make sure to rub a little butter or apply some cooking spray to the exposed rods, as they aren't coated in nonstick lining and will adhere to your baked bread.

- → **After shaping:** What's known as the bulk rise is the first stage of letting the yeast do its thing, whereas "proofing" is what happens once it's in its final rising stage, after the dough has been shaped. After shaping your bread, return it to the bread machine's baking pan (or to a traditional loaf pan, if you intend to bake it in your home oven), and proof it covered, in the refrigerator, then bake it off the next morning. Allow 30 to 60 minutes for the proofed dough to warm up first.

For a More Golden-Brown Crust

Most bread machines don't have a heating element in the upper part of their compartments, which means that they often come out with a bit of a pale crust. You can mitigate this by brushing a little egg white or other type of wash over the surface of the dough after it completes its final proof.

Using one of the Crust-Browning Washes below, gently brush the entire top surface of the dough when it's almost finished proofing, usually about 1 hour 30 minutes before completion. Your timing doesn't have to be perfect—either toward the end of the final proof or even the beginning of baking works just fine. My preference is an egg white, because I often have a leftover egg white or a carton of packaged egg whites on hand, and I love the glossy sheen it adds.

Crust-Browning Washes

All of these washes are the amount needed for 1 loaf.

- → **Egg white:** About 1 scant tablespoon egg white
- → **Egg wash:** About 2 teaspoons beaten egg whisked with 1 teaspoon water
- → **Milk wash:** About 1 scant tablespoon whole milk or unflavored plant-based milk, preferably a higher-protein one like soy milk or oat milk
- → **Starch slurry:** 1 teaspoon cornstarch, potato starch, or arrowroot whisked with 1 tablespoon tepid water
- → **Melted butter or oil:** About 1 scant tablespoon

The Breadmaking Process, Step by Step

1 Mixing and Kneading

First, your bread's ingredients are combined and moistened, and will look a bit shaggy. Then kneading begins, during which the dough is thoroughly stretched out over and over again, with the goal of strengthening the gluten in the wheat. It becomes elastic in the process, so that the dough can inflate with bubbles without tearing—creating the architecture of the baked bread's crumb. Through kneading, the dough becomes smooth, somewhat shiny, and is ideally just a bit tacky, meaning that it should stick to a pan or work surface temporarily, but then cleanly release.

2 Bulk Fermentation

During bulk fermentation, or the first rise, the yeast begins its work on the dough, interacting with its sugars to produce gas in the form of carbon dioxide and ethanol. It bubbles up inside the dough and causes the whole mass to inflate, roughly doubling its size in volume. Bulk fermentation should take place in a relatively warm environment, around 80°F, which the bread machine creates perfectly.

3 Deflation, or Punch-Down

After the dough doubles in size, it's deflated, or punched down (when making it by hand, you can literally punch the dough down). This works the gluten and helps to prevent the dough from overinflating, and also helps to yield evenly sized bubbles. In bread machines, there is usually a second bulk fermentation (second rise) and punch-down.

4 Shaping

Once the bulk fermentation stages are complete, the dough is ready to be shaped. Some bread machines have a special function for shaping the dough into a loaf, others simply leave it in the shape of the punched-down dough.

But for things like dinner rolls and cinnamon buns, or if you plan to bake your bread in your home oven, this is when the dough is removed from the machine and handled.

5 Proofing

Proofing is the final stage of fermentation, where the shaped dough is left to inflate and double in size once more, to develop its final crumb structure before the higher heat of an oven (or a bread machine's bake function) is applied and locks everything in place.

6 Baking

This is last stage, the application of high heat. During baking the yeast is killed, but not before it uses its last gasp to puff up a little bit more (known in baking parlance as "oven spring"), giving the loaf a final injection of volume. The moisture in the dough is largely evaporated off, leaving behind a light, airy loaf of bread with a complicated interior network of bubbles, otherwise known as its "crumb." To preserve the structure of the bread, hold off slicing into it before it has cooled down.

For a More Attractive, Hand-Shaped Loaf

Shaping dough by hand is the best way to ensure an attractive loaf. It's also easy, quick, and not very messy—especially if you resist the urge to use extra flour while handling it. If baking your loaf in the bread machine, you'll need to pay attention to when its final rise occurs so that you can intervene at the right moment (the machine's manual may help here). After its final punch-down occurs, pause the bread machine cycle and remove the dough from the machine.

1. On a clean work surface, gently stretch the dough out into a rough rectangle shape about an inch thick. Avoid adding extra flour here unless it's absolutely necessary, using a bench scraper instead to help handle and lift the dough.
2. Fold the bottom third of the dough into the middle (2nd photo), then fold in the left and right ends to the middle (3rd photo).
3. Now tightly roll the dough over the top flap. It should look like a log (4th photo).
4. Flip the dough over and use your fingers to pinch the seams together so that they seal.

Return the shaped loaf to the bread machine, seam-side down, and resume the cycle, or place it in a greased loaf pan for baking in a home oven (see page 33 for more info).

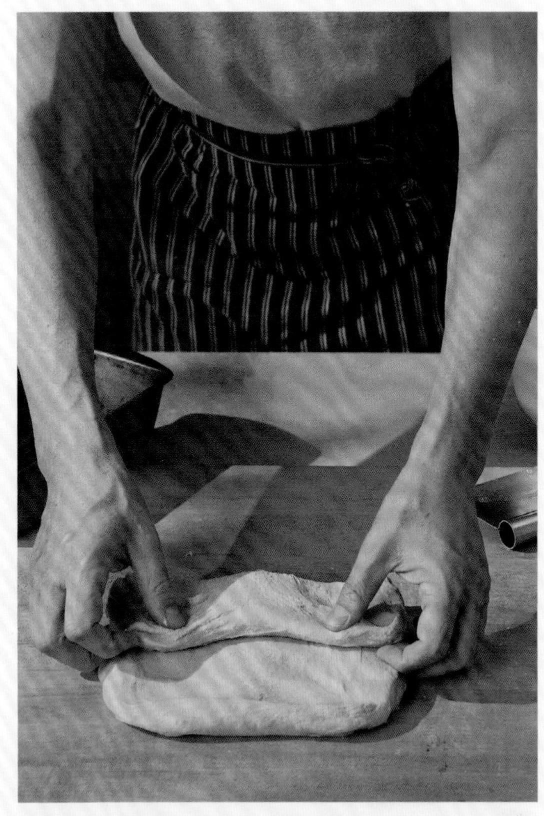

To Incorporate Mix-Ins and Swirls

Many bread machines have a built-in alert or special compartment for additions like nuts, fruit, chocolate, or cheese—typically an alarm goes off about 5 minutes before kneading is complete, or a trap door opens and releases them into the dough. Sometimes this works, but I've found that the additions aren't always evenly distributed, so I usually opt to incorporate them manually.

1. After the dough's first bulk fermentation (first rise), pause the machine and remove the dough.
2. On a clean work surface, pat the dough out to an even thickness of about an inch. Sprinkle one-third of the fillings over the dough, then roll it up tightly jelly-roll style, or fold the dough over itself. Use a bench scraper to help maneuver the dough.
3. Flatten it out again, sprinkle another third of the fillings over it, and roll or fold it.
4. Repeat one last time, incorporating the final portion of fillings. Shape the dough into a loaf, return it to the bread machine, and resume its cycle.

To Bake in a Home Oven

All of these loaves can be baked in a home oven instead of the bread machine, which is a great option if you prefer a loaf that doesn't have any paddle holes.

1. Remove the dough from the machine after it has completed its bulk fermentation, just before shaping and proofing take place. Shape it into a loaf and proof it in a greased loaf pan.
2. Preheat the oven to 350°F, using convection if available. (If you have convection, it will simply spread the heat more evenly throughout the oven by the use of a fan, and is great for getting even browning on crusts. But if you don't have convection, don't sweat it.)

3. If desired, brush the bread with egg white or other crust-browning wash (see page 26) and score the bread by making one long slash, or a few diagonal ones, down the length of the loaf using a sharp knife. This is also the opportunity to sprinkle the crust with any decorative garnishes, such as seeds or oats.
4. Bake until it sounds hollow when tapped on the top, 40 to 50 minutes. If you want to be extra precise with doneness, use an instant-read thermometer to check that the center of the loaf has reached 190°F. Note that if you use a glass or Pyrex loaf pan, you'll need to add an extra 10 to 20 minutes of baking time, because the thicker glass slows down the heat from reaching the center of the bread.

A Few Helpful Tools

→ **A digital scale:** It bears repeating! There are inexpensive ones available for $12 to $15, but my favorite is the Oxo stainless steel scale, which has a capacity of 11 pounds and a pull-out digital display. It's sturdier than the inexpensive plastic ones, and the pull-out display is always easy to read because there's no worry that the lip of a mixing bowl will block the view.

→ **Small flexible spatula:** The mini "spoonula" from GIR is particularly helpful for scraping against the sides, corners, and bottom of a bread machine baking pan and for removing proofed dough, too.

→ **Bench scraper:** If you plan to shape loaves by hand, a bench scraper seriously helps for handling the dough and getting beneath it, avoiding the need for adding any unnecessary extra flour.

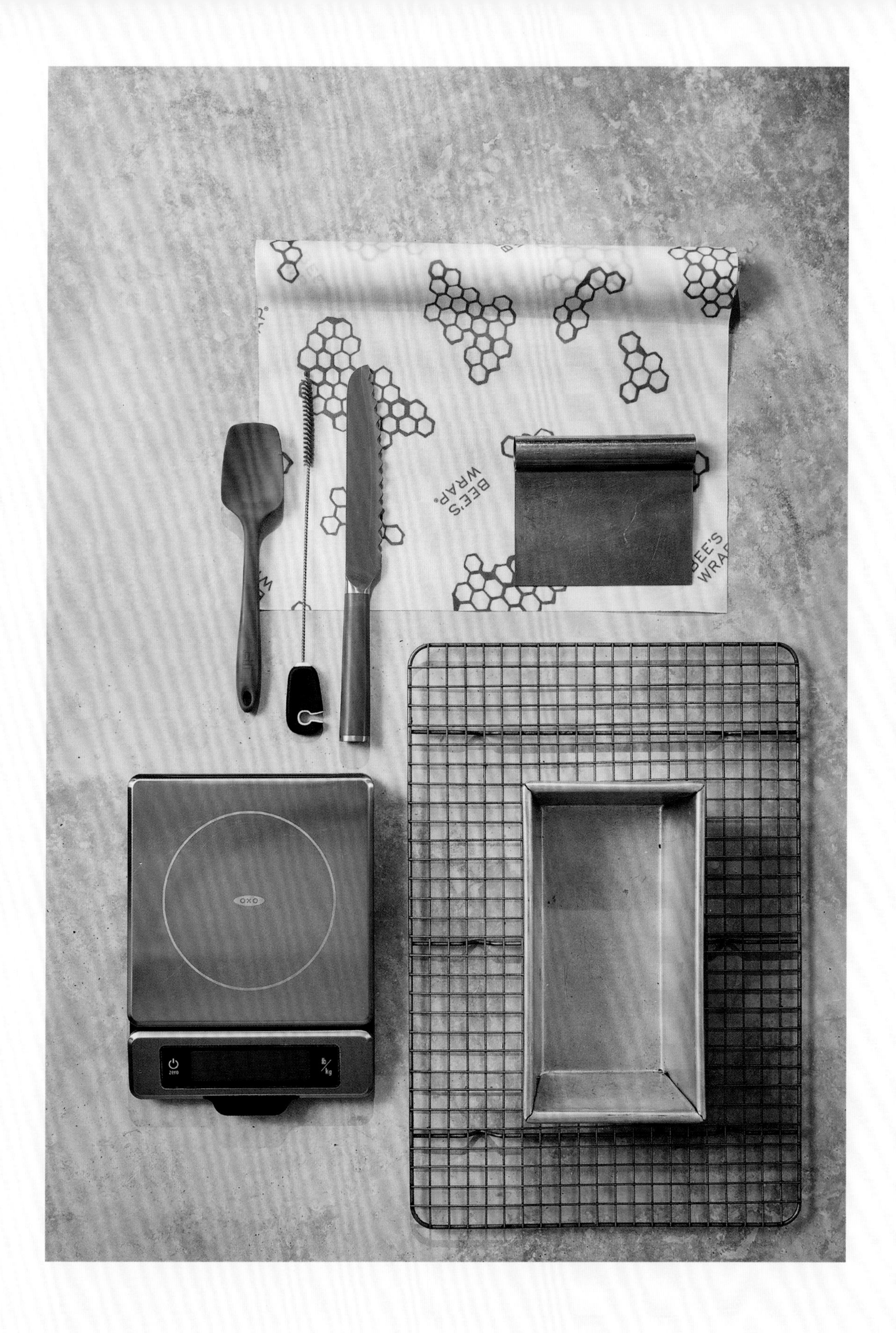
BEE'S WRAP®
BEE'S WRAP
OXO
zero
lb/kg

→ **Reusable food wrap:** Wax-lined food wrap, which can be used over and over again, comes in handy for covering the pan and proofing dough overnight in the fridge. I also like it for wrapping up leftover bread, because it molds nicely around any shape of loaf.

→ **Cooling rack:** Avoid letting baked bread cool inside the bread machine. Instead, tip it out onto a cooling rack. An 8½ × 12-inch "quarter sheet cooling rack" (half the size of a standard sheet pan) is the perfect size for cooling a bread machine loaf.

→ **A good serrated knife:** For even, smooth slices of fresh bread, a good serrated knife is essential. It should be sharp, a little bit heavy, and glide through the bread in smooth, even strokes. A subpar knife will require force, squishing your beautiful bread.

→ **Straw cleaner:** Bits of dough tend to get caked inside the hole in bread machine paddles, especially with wetter doughs, and a straw cleaner makes it easy to scrub it away. Oxo makes one that comes with their water bottle cleaning set, or you can pick up a package at a craft store.

→ **Metal loaf pan:** For shaping dough by hand and baking it in your home oven, the best loaf pan for these recipes is the larger capacity 9 × 5 × 3-inch size. Smaller standard sized ones (8½ × 4½ inches) will also do, but the bread may balloon over the sides a little bit. Opt for metal over glass, as glass requires extra cooking time and can throw off proofing because it takes longer to heat up and cool down.

Key Ingredients

Flour

Use bread making as an opportunity to expand your palate and pantry. While these recipes stick to readily available flours that behave consistently in the bread machine, your baking practice will be enriched by experimenting with lesser-known and locally sourced flours.

→ **Bread flour, strong white flour, or high-protein flour:** The higher the proportion of protein in the flour, the stronger the gluten development will be in the finished loaves. My go-to is King Arthur's Unbleached Bread Flour, which has a protein content of about 12.7%, but any bread flour in the 12% to 14% range will work great.

→ **Whole wheat flour:** Many recipes here incorporate whole wheat flour, which adds flavor, texture (in the form of little flecks of bran), and a more robust nutritional profile to a loaf of bread. For more of a true "whole wheat" flour, look for "stone-milled" flour, in which all of the edible wheat grain's bran, germ, and endosperm are ground up together, unlike many supermarket options in which a portion of bran is separately mixed into all-purpose white flour. Most whole wheat flour is made from a variety called "red" whole wheat, but **white whole wheat flour** can be used interchangeably. It's widely available in the King Arthur brand and has the same nutritional profile of whole wheat flour, but it imparts a lighter color to the finished loaves.

→ **Other specialty flours:** Other types of flours add character to loaves, as you'll see here.

  → **Whole wheat pastry flour:** Milled to a softer consistency than standard whole wheat flour, this can be easily substituted for 25% to 30% of the bread flour called for in any of these recipes; it's particularly good for tender baked goods like

STARDUST
WHOLE WHEAT
BARTON SPRINGS MILL
RYE
ORGANIC RYE FLOUR
MAINE GRAINS.
For Full Flavored Breads
HAYDEN
FLOUR MILLS
Heritage Bread Wheat
ARTISAN BREAD FLOUR
KING ARTHUR BAKING COMPANY
WHOLE WHEAT FLOUR BLEND
REGENERATIVELY-GROWN
RESTORE SOIL HEALTH
12.7%

cinnamon buns or dinner rolls, adding toasty flavor and a bit of color.

    - → **Spelt flour:** The nutty flavor of this flour is a favorite, too, though it has a lower protein content than whole wheat, which can affect the crumb structure and limit how much the bread rises.
    - → **Rye flour:** This is incredibly useful for maintaining your sourdough starter, as well as adding delicious earthiness to certain loaves.
    - → **Barley flour:** A tender flour that gives a sweet, slightly malty flavor and a bit of earthy texture to soft loaves, such as the Honey-Barley Milk Bread (page 77).
    - → **Gluten-free options:** Flours such as **buckwheat, oat** (certified gluten-free, if necessary), and **almond** all come into play in these pages as well.

- → **Local grains:** I encourage you to explore your local grains, either at your farmers' market or by doing a quick Internet search. The local grains movement has been instrumental in combating the detrimental effects of monoculture crops (subsidized wheat, corn, and soy) that strip nutrients from soil and destroy the biodiversity of a region, by reintroducing regenerative farming practices. To achieve consistent results, in these recipes I typically substitute just a portion of local grain—25% to 30%—for some of the bread flour, or in whole wheat breads, use something similar to whole wheat flour (such as a local spelt flour) for the whole wheat flour.

How to Make Bread Flour from All-Purpose Flour

Make your own bread flour from all-purpose flour by mixing in a bit of vital wheat gluten, or wheat protein. For one cup of bread flour, combine 125g (1 cup minus 2 teaspoons) all-purpose flour with 5g (2 teaspoons) of vital wheat gluten.

Yeast

Instant yeast (which can also be labeled "Bread Machine Yeast") is the best choice for these recipes because it works a bit more quickly than active dry yeast, and bread machines are better optimized for it than active dry. If you plan to bake bread with any frequency, I recommend buying a 1-pound pouch of SAF-Instant yeast, transferring it to a clean 1-quart jar, and storing it in the refrigerator, where it'll keep for a good long time.

If you only have active dry yeast, you can use that, too. Contrary to popular belief, it doesn't need to be proofed before mixing it into a dough—that step simply ensures that the yeast is fresh and alive. So, if active dry is all you've got, you can use it, but you may want to keep tabs on it during proofing, intervening to allow more time if necessary.

Salt

If you use a digital scale in your baking (which I hope you do!), then it doesn't matter what kind of salt you use in these recipes—simply follow the gram weight. If you plan to measure by volume, then you'll need to pay closer attention, because different types of salt have different densities, with the same volume measurements weighing different amounts. This can impart vastly different levels of saltiness in food.

I've made fine sea salt the default here—I know that Diamond Crystal kosher salt is popular among professional cooks, but fine sea salt is easier to find for home cooks and more versatile in recipes, weighing essentially the same as table salt and Morton kosher salt. If using Diamond Crystal kosher salt and you can't go by weight, double the volume.

Quick Salt Conversion

2 teaspoons Diamond Crystal kosher salt = 1 teaspoon fine sea salt or Morton kosher salt

Eggs

In the recipes where eggs appear, I always use large eggs, which usually weigh 50 grams. They primarily appear in enriched loaves like brioche or the dough for Choose-Your-Own-Adventure Swirl Bread (page 123), where they help not to bind, as is the case in other types of baking, but to provide structure in a relatively heavy, rich dough. The protein in egg whites adds strength as the loaf bakes, and the yolks add to the overall richness of the bread.

If you don't eat eggs, the best approach is simply to eliminate them, since in many breads they aren't needed (I've included veganizing options with the recipes where applicable). But I also adjust the liquid component: A large egg yolk usually weighs 18g and the white about 32g. Since the white is where most of the egg's water is, that's what I focus on making up for. So, start by adding an extra 30g (2 tablespoons) of water or nondairy milk and 2 teaspoons of oil (avocado or olive, depending on the flavor I'm after) to the dough and as it kneads, keep an eye on the hydration, adding additional liquid or flour bit by bit until a soft but relatively sturdy dough takes shape.

Sweeteners

Bread machine recipes benefit from a bit of additional sugar in the dough, because this helps them to develop a darker crust and have a more rounded flavor given the quick proofing and baking time. Sweeteners are largely interchangeable in bread when used in small amounts. If a recipe calls for less than 2 tablespoons, use any sweetener you like. But if there's any more than that, you can't substitute a liquid sweetener for a dry one, or it will mess with the hydration of the dough.

→ For liquid sweeteners: I like **honey** (I prefer a runny one, which is easier to measure), **maple syrup**, and **molasses**.

→ **For dry sweeteners:** You'll find **coconut sugar** (I love its slight savoriness), **brown sugar** (dark or light are used interchangeably here), and **organic granulated sugar** appear most frequently.

Fats

Bread machine recipes also benefit from a bit of fat in the dough, for the same reason that they need a little sugar: for color and for flavor. **Butter** or **vegan butter** (such as the Miyoko's brand), **extra-virgin olive oil,** and **avocado oil** are my primary fats of choice. Vegetable and canola oil can be used in place of avocado oil, too.

No-Stress Substitutions

Baking is more flexible than many people realize, and substitutions can often be made without causing significant issues. But if you make changes, monitor the dough as it kneads, adding either a bit more flour or liquid in the event that a new ingredient affects the dough's hydration.

If the recipe calls for . . .	You can substitute . . .	But know that . . .
Bread flour	All-purpose flour, by weight	The bread may rise less, due to there being less gluten in all-purpose flour.
Bread flour and no additional whole-grain flour in the recipe	Up to 25% whole-grain flour, such as spelt or barley, by weight	The flecks of bran in whole-grain flour will affect the texture, and with less gluten in whole-grain flours, the loaf will rise less. Monitor the dough as it's kneading, adding additional liquid if too dry.
Whole wheat flour in addition to bread flour in the recipe	Spelt flour, by weight	Spelt has a bit less gluten than whole wheat flour, so the bread may rise a little less.
Whole wheat flour in a 100% whole wheat recipe	Up to 25% whole-grain flour, such as spelt or barley, by weight	Nothing to worry about!
Spelt flour, in addition to other flours	Whole wheat or barley flour, by weight	Nothing to worry about!
Less than 2 tablespoons dry sweetener (white or brown sugar, coconut sugar)	Liquid sweetener like honey or maple syrup, by weight	Nothing to worry about!
Less than 2 tablespoons liquid sweetener (honey, maple syrup)	Granulated white sugar, brown sugar, or coconut sugar	Nothing to worry about!
Eggs	3 tablespoons water plus 2 teaspoons avocado or olive oil	The bread may rise less, and the crust will be lighter. Monitor the hydration of the dough as it kneads, adding additional flour if needed.
Dairy milk	Nondairy milk	The dough may not be quite as tender but will still be good. A higher-protein milk such as soy milk will perform best.
Less than 3 tablespoons oil (avocado, olive oil)	Soft unsalted butter or vegan butter, by weight	The flavor will be affected but the texture will be fine.
Less than 3 tablespoons butter	Oil (avocado, olive), by volume	Monitor the hydration of the dough as it kneads, adding additional flour if needed.

A Few Final Recommendations

Storing Leftover Bread

It's no secret that most homemade bread is best eaten within 24 to 48 hours. When storing at room temperature overnight, avoid airtight containers, which make the crust chewy and can even accelerate molding. Instead, use a clean paper bag, or wrap the loaf in reusable food wrap or foil. And to keep it longer, slice the cooled bread, pack it into an airtight bag or container, and freeze it. It can be toasted directly out of the freezer, or will thaw at room temperature in about 20 minutes.

Cleaning Your Bread Machine

While every bread machine pan I've encountered is coated in a nonstick lining that makes for easy cleaning, dough tends to get trapped around the kneading paddle as it mixes, and can expand in between the rod and the paddle during baking. Occasionally, this results in the kneading paddle getting baked into the pan, making it difficult to remove. To avoid this situation, fill the pan with an inch or two of water as soon as you remove a baked loaf, which will soften any stuck bits.

And while many bread machine manuals claim that their baking pans are dishwasher safe, stick with hand-washing. As is the case with nonstick skillets, the dishwasher can damage the pan's lining, causing it to scratch, chip, or flake away. And besides, they're quick and easy to hand-wash with hot, soapy water and a soft sponge.

Over time, the inner chamber of the bread machine may collect stray bits of flour and other grains. Use a clean, moist towel to occasionally wipe away the debris while the machine is turned off and cooled down.

Baking at High Elevation

While these recipes have been perfected at low elevation (close to sea level or below 1,000 feet), I've also made most of them at about 7,500 feet, in the mountains around Lake Tahoe in Nevada. In general, elevation can cause bread to rise 50 percent faster (or more!) and in a bread machine, which isn't equipped for such variance, your loaves are almost guaranteed to overproof and then tragically collapse, leaving a crater in their centers. To bake these recipes at high elevation, opt for the second, "Hand-Shaped" method that's included in the recipes, so that you can monitor the second rise before baking. This is a little bit of extra work, but your bread will thank you.

2

Everyday Classics

Go-to breads that enhance everyday eating: Soft sandwich loaves for packed-lunch PB&Js, hearty whole-grain loaves for avocado toasts and dunking into weeknight soups, and fuss-free recipes that integrate into hectic lives.

Half-Wheat Sandwich Loaf

This is a simple, everyday loaf for baking once or twice a week to suit your default bread needs. It's soft and squishy enough to please kids, but with enough whole-grain goodness to appease the adults, too. A good-quality whole wheat flour will define its flavor and texture, adding flecks of bran throughout the loaf.

Makes 1 loaf

Ingredient	Grams	Volume
Whole milk or plant-based milk	180g	3/4 cup
Tepid water	160g	2/3 cup
Brown sugar or coconut sugar	28g	2 tablespoons
Fine sea salt	10g	1 1/2 teaspoons
Bread flour	260g	2 cups, spooned and leveled
Whole wheat or white whole wheat flour	245g	1 3/4 cups, spooned and leveled
Softened unsalted butter or vegan butter, cut into cubes	28g	2 tablespoons
Instant yeast	—	2 teaspoons
Egg white or other crust-browning wash (optional; see page 26)	—	—

Hands-Off Method

In the order listed, add all the ingredients (except for the egg white) to the bread machine's baking pan. Program the machine to its **WHEAT** setting and **MEDIUM** or **DARK** crust. Lock the pan into the machine, close the lid, and press **START**. If desired, after the loaf's final rise (usually around 1:30 from completion), pause the program and brush the proofed loaf with egg white. Once complete, remove the bread from the machine and let cool in the pan for 10 to 15 minutes. Then tip the loaf out of the pan onto a cooling rack to cool completely before slicing.

Hand-Shaped Method

In the order listed, add all the ingredients (except for the egg white) to the bread machine's baking pan. Select **DOUGH**, lock the pan into the machine, close the lid, and press **START**. At the completion of the cycle,

continued →

Half-Wheat Sandwich Loaf

continued

the dough should be doubled in size; if not, leave it in the machine for additional time as needed.

Transfer the dough to a clean work surface. If it's too sticky to handle, dust it lightly with flour, but resist adding any more than necessary, and use a bench scraper to help lift and move it around. Gently stretch it to a thickness of about 1 inch, then shape it to fit a 9 × 5-inch loaf pan (see page 30, for tips) if baking in a home oven.

Place the loaf seam-side down back in the bread machine pan (or in a greased loaf pan if baking in a home oven). Close the bread machine lid and proof in the bread machine (or cover the loaf pan with a clean towel or food wrap and proof in a warm spot in the kitchen) until doubled in size, about 1 hour. You can also proof the dough overnight in the refrigerator; allow it to warm up at room temperature for 30 to 60 minutes before baking.

To bake in a bread machine: If desired, brush the top of the loaf with egg white and lock the pan into the bread machine. Select the **BAKE** setting and bake the loaf for 1 hour. Remove the pan from the machine and allow the bread to cool in the pan for 15 minutes. Then tip out onto a cooling rack to cool completely before slicing.

To bake in a home oven: Preheat the oven to 350°F, using convection if available. If desired, brush the top of the loaf with egg white and score the bread by making a long slash down the length of the loaf with a sharp knife. Bake until browned and hollow-sounding when you tap on the loaf or an instant-read thermometer reads 190°F, 40 to 50 minutes. Cool in the pan for at least 15 minutes. Then tip out onto a cooling rack to cool completely before slicing.

Leftovers and Storage: Keeps for up to 2 days at room temperature, wrapped loosely. Stored in an airtight bag or container, the sliced loaf can be frozen for up to 1 month.

Soft White Sandwich Loaf

No bread cookbook is complete without a plush, butter-scented, pure white sandwich bread, and the bread machine makes it easy to turn out such a loaf at a moment's notice. You'll want this for your peanut butter and jellies, to soak up the juices of your ripest summer tomatoes, and it's a good choice for a Croque Fill-in-the-Blank (page 197) as well. Leftovers make excellent all-purpose bread crumbs (see page 196).

Makes 1 loaf

Ingredient	Grams	Volume
Tepid water	240g	1 cup
Whole milk or plant-based milk	80g	1/3 cup
Maple syrup	42g	2 tablespoons
Fine sea salt	10g	1 1/2 teaspoons
Bread flour	480g	3 3/4 cups, spooned and leveled
Unsalted butter or vegan butter, cut into cubes, at room temperature	42g	3 tablespoons
Instant yeast	—	2 teaspoons
Egg white or other crust-browning wash (optional; see page 26)	—	—

Hands-Off Method

In the order listed, add all the ingredients (except for the egg white) to the bread machine's baking pan. Program the machine to its WHITE setting and MEDIUM crust. Lock the pan into the machine, close the lid, and press START. If desired, after the loaf's final rise (usually around 1:30 from completion), pause the program and brush the proofed loaf with egg white. Once complete, remove the bread from the machine and let cool in the pan for 10 to 15 minutes. Then tip the loaf out of the pan onto a cooling rack to cool completely before slicing.

Hand-Shaped Method

In the order listed, add all the ingredients (except for the egg white) to the bread machine's

continued →

Soft White Sandwich Loaf
continued

baking pan. Select **DOUGH**, lock the pan into the machine, close the lid, and press **START**. At the completion of the cycle, the dough should be doubled in size; if not, leave it in the machine for additional time as needed.

Transfer the dough to a clean work surface. If it's too sticky to handle, dust it lightly with flour, but resist adding any more than necessary, and use a bench scraper to help lift and move it around. Gently stretch it to a thickness of about 1 inch, then shape it to fit a 9 × 5-inch loaf pan (see page 30, for tips) if baking in a home oven.

Place the loaf seam-side down back in the bread machine pan (or in a greased loaf pan if baking in a home oven). Close the bread machine lid and proof in the bread machine (or cover the loaf pan with a clean towel or food wrap and proof in a warm spot in the kitchen) until doubled in size, about 1 hour. You can also proof the dough overnight in the refrigerator; allow it to warm up at room temperature for 30 to 60 minutes before baking.

To bake in a bread machine: If desired, brush the top of the loaf with egg white, and lock the pan into the bread machine. Select the **BAKE** setting and bake the loaf for 1 hour. Remove the pan from the machine and allow the bread to cool in the pan for 15 minutes. Then tip out onto a cooling rack to cool completely before slicing.

To bake in a home oven: Preheat the oven to 350°F, using convection if available. If desired, brush the top of the loaf with egg white and score the bread by making a long slash down the length of the loaf with a sharp knife. Bake until browned and hollow-sounding when you tap on the loaf or an instant-read thermometer reads 190°F, 40 to 50 minutes. Cool in the pan for at least 15 minutes. Then tip the loaf out onto a cooling rack to cool completely before slicing.

Leftovers and Storage: Keeps for up to 2 days, wrapped loosely at room temperature. Stored in an airtight bag or container, the sliced loaf can be frozen for up to 1 month.

Honey Whole Wheat Loaf

A classic wheat loaf for deli-style sandwiches, this has a mildly sweet and toasty flavor, a tender crumb, and a nice dark color thanks to a drizzle of molasses. Because of the bran in whole wheat flour, it always benefits from more time to hydrate, so I start this recipe with an "autolyse," which is just the process of combining the water and (most of) the flour to hydrate for a few hours, before kneading in the remaining ingredients.

Makes 1 loaf

Ingredient	Grams	Volume
Autolyse		
Whole wheat or white whole wheat flour	350g	2½ cups, spooned and leveled
Tepid water	300g	1¼ cups
Dough		
Whole wheat or white whole wheat flour	105g	¾ cup, spooned and leveled
Honey	60g	3 tablespoons
Olive oil	33g	3 tablespoons
Fine sea salt	10g	1½ teaspoons
Molasses	7g	1 teaspoon
Instant yeast	—	2 teaspoons
Egg white or other crust-browning wash (optional; see page 26)	—	—

Prepare the Autolyse: Combine the flour and water in the bread machine's baking pan. Select or create a custom program to **KNEAD** for 5 minutes (or start any program, then set your timer for 5 minutes), and press **START**. After the 5 minutes, turn off the machine. Use a flexible spatula to smooth the paste into an even layer and tidy up the sides of the pan, and leave the dough to rest in the machine, covered, for 2 to 3 hours, during which time the mixture will relax and loosen a bit.

continued →

Honey Whole Wheat Loaf

continued

Hands-Off Method

Add all the ingredients except for the egg white to the autolyse in the order listed. Program the machine to its **WHEAT** setting and **MEDIUM** or **DARK** crust. Lock the pan into the machine, close the lid, and press **START**. If desired, after the loaf's final rise (usually around 1:30 from completion), pause the program and brush the proofed loaf with egg white. Once complete, remove the bread from the machine and let cool in the pan for 10 to 15 minutes. Then tip out of the pan onto a cooling rack to cool completely before slicing.

Hand-Shaped Method

Add all the remaining ingredients except for the egg white to the autolyse in the order listed. Select **DOUGH**, lock the pan into the machine, close the lid, and press **START**. At the completion of the cycle, the dough should be doubled in size; if not, leave it in the machine for additional time as needed.

Transfer the dough to a clean work surface. If it's too sticky to handle, dust it lightly with flour, but resist adding any more than necessary, and use a bench scraper to help lift and move it around. Gently stretch it to a thickness of about 1 inch, then shape it to fit a 9 × 5-inch loaf pan (see page 30, for tips) if baking in a home oven.

Place the loaf seam-side down back in the bread machine pan (or in a greased loaf pan if baking in a home oven). Close the bread machine lid and proof in the bread machine (or cover the loaf pan with a clean towel or food wrap and proof in a warm spot in the kitchen) until doubled in size, about 1 hour. You can also proof the dough overnight in the refrigerator; allow it to warm up at room temperature for 30 to 60 minutes before baking.

To bake in a bread machine: If desired, brush the top of the loaf with egg white, and lock the pan into the bread machine. Select the **BAKE** setting and bake the loaf for 1 hour. Remove the pan from the machine and allow the bread to cool in the pan for 15 minutes. Then tip the loaf out onto a cooling rack to cool completely before slicing.

To bake in a home oven: Preheat the oven to 350°F, using convection if available. If desired, brush the top of the loaf with egg white and score the bread by making a long slash down the length of the loaf with a sharp knife. Bake until browned and hollow-sounding when you tap on the loaf or an instant-read thermometer reads 190°F, 40 to 50 minutes. Let the bread cool in the pan for at least 15 minutes. Then tip out onto a cooling rack to cool completely before slicing.

Leftovers and Storage: Keeps for up to 2 days, wrapped loosely at room temperature. Stored in an airtight bag or container, the sliced loaf can be frozen for up to 1 month.

Buttermilk Oat & Wheat Loaf

A relatively small amount of buttermilk adds not just tang to breads, but it makes them a bit more tender and aerated, its acidity breaking down the proteins in flour to produce a moist and craggy crumb. This loaf is a favorite for butter and jam. Use instant (or quick-cooking) oats if possible, because they'll blend more seamlessly into the dough; if you opt for thicker-cut oats, go by weight; you'll need about 10% less of the volume.

Makes 1 loaf

Ingredient	Grams	Volume
Tepid water	240g	1 cup
Buttermilk	120g	1/2 cup
Egg	50g	1 large
Honey or maple syrup	40g	2 tablespoons
Extra-virgin olive oil	33g	3 tablespoons
Fine sea salt	10g	1 1/2 teaspoons
Whole wheat or white whole wheat flour	420g	3 cups, spooned and leveled
Instant or quick-cooking oats, plus extra for sprinkling	100g	1 cup
Instant yeast	—	2 teaspoons
Egg white or other crust-browning wash (optional; see page 26)	—	—

Hands-Off Method

In the order listed, add all the ingredients (except for the egg white) to the bread machine's baking pan. Program the machine to its **WHEAT** setting and **MEDIUM** or **DARK** crust. Lock the pan into the machine, close the lid, and press **START**. If desired, after the loaf's final rise (usually around 1:30 from completion), pause the program and brush the proofed loaf with egg white and sprinkle with additional oats. Once complete, remove the bread

continued →

from the machine and let cool in the pan for 10 to 15 minutes. Then tip the loaf out of the pan onto a cooling rack to cool completely before slicing.

Hand-Shaped Method

In the order listed, add all the ingredients (except for the egg white) to the bread machine's baking pan. Select **DOUGH**, lock the pan into the machine, close the lid, and press **START**. At the completion of the cycle, the dough should be doubled in size; if not, leave it in the machine for additional time as needed.

Transfer the dough to a clean work surface. If it's too sticky to handle, dust it lightly with flour, but resist adding any more than necessary, and use a bench scraper to help lift and move it around. Gently stretch it to a thickness of about 1 inch, then shape it to fit a 9 × 5-inch loaf pan (see page 30, for tips) if baking in a home oven.

Place the loaf seam-side down back in the bread machine pan (or in a greased loaf pan if baking in a home oven). Close the bread machine lid and proof in the bread machine (or cover the loaf pan with a clean towel or food wrap and proof in a warm spot in the kitchen) until doubled in size, about 1 hour. You can also proof the dough overnight in the refrigerator; allow it to warm up at room temperature for 30 to 60 minutes before baking.

To bake in a bread machine: If desired, brush the top of the loaf with egg white, sprinkle with additional oats, and lock the pan into the bread machine. Select the **BAKE** setting and bake the loaf for 1 hour. Remove the pan from the machine and allow the bread to cool in the pan for 15 minutes. Then tip out onto a cooling rack to cool completely before slicing.

To bake in a home oven: Preheat the oven to 350°F, using convection if available. If desired, brush the top of the loaf with egg white and sprinkle with additional oats, and score the bread by making a long slash down the length of the loaf with a sharp knife. Bake until browned and hollow-sounding when you tap on the loaf or an instant-read thermometer reads 190°F, 40 to 50 minutes. Cool in the pan for at least 15 minutes. Then tip out onto a cooling rack to cool completely before slicing.

Leftovers and Storage: Keeps for up to 2 days, wrapped loosely at room temperature. Stored in an airtight bag or container, the sliced loaf can be frozen for up to 1 month.

Variation

Vegan Oat & Wheat Loaf: Substitute plain nondairy yogurt (not Greek-style) for the buttermilk, and replace the egg with 30g (2 tablespoons) water and 8g (2 teaspoons) olive oil.

Gluten-Free Toasting Bread

Punch-downs aren't really necessary in gluten-free bread, since that step is designed to help strengthen the gluten in wheat flour. Yet bread machines commonly include them in their Gluten-Free cycles, which I find yields a deflated and dense loaf. So as a workaround, I isolate the mixing and baking functions when I make gluten-free loaves. This lightly sweet, versatile recipe uses a store-bought GF flour blend, along with psyllium husk (a natural, soluble fiber that adds stretchiness), and has wiggle room in the form of a few options for additional flours to customize it. It's a squatter loaf than others, but has a wonderful flavor and is a terrific base for all manner of toast toppings.

Makes 1 loaf

Ingredient	Grams	Volume
Whole milk	320g	1⅓ cups
Egg whites	100g	3 large
Brown sugar or coconut sugar	41g	3 tablespoons
Apple cider vinegar or distilled white vinegar	13g	2 teaspoons
Fine sea salt	10g	1½ teaspoons
Extra-virgin olive oil or avocado oil	22g	2 tablespoons
Gluten-free flour blend (see Note)	338g	2½ cups, spooned and leveled
Buckwheat flour (or oat or almond flour, see Variation, page 64)	70g	½ cup, spooned and leveled
Psyllium husk powder	12g	1 tablespoon
Instant yeast	—	2 teaspoons
Egg white or other crust-browning wash (optional; see page 26)	—	—

continued →

Gluten-Free Toasting Bread

continued

Add all the ingredients except the crust-browning wash to the bread machine's baking pan in the order listed. Select **DOUGH**, or create a custom setting to **KNEAD** the mixture for 5 minutes, if your machine has custom features. Lock the pan into the machine, close the lid, and press **START**. Once the mixture is combined, after about 5 minutes, halt the program and turn off the machine. Use a flexible spatula to tidy up the edges of the pan and smooth the top.

Leave the dough to proof until it roughly doubles in size, usually 1 hour 15 minutes to 2 hours.

If desired, brush the top of the proofed loaf with crust-browning wash and lock the pan into the bread machine. Select the **BAKE** setting and bake the loaf for 1 hour. Remove the pan from the machine and allow the bread to cool in the pan for 10 to 15 minutes. Then tip out onto a cooling rack to cool completely before slicing.

Leftovers and Storage: Keeps for up to 3 days, wrapped loosely at room temperature. Stored in an airtight bag or container, the sliced loaf can be frozen for up to 1 month.

Note: A gluten-free flour blend that includes xanthan gum will yield a more open crumb in this recipe.

Variation

Oat or Almond GF Bread: For an oat or almond profile in your loaf, substitute 70g (2/3 cup) certified gluten-free oat flour or 70g (scant 3/4 cup) superfine almond flour for the buckwheat flour.

Buttery Brioche

Pushing the limits of what a buttery, fluffy, and magnificently bronzed loaf can be, brioche is traditionally made by adding softened butter bit by bit to the kneading dough. But in a bread machine you can pile everything in all at once and step away, making this one of the most hands-free versions there might be. While brioche dries out quickly, it is leftovers "gold," taking on new glory in grilled sandwiches, soaked in custard for French Toast (page 198) or Bread Pudding (page 197), or used as croutons in tomato soup.

Makes 1 loaf

Ingredient	Grams	Volume
Whole milk	180g	3/4 cup
Eggs	100g	2 large
Honey	60g	3 tablespoons
Fine sea salt	10g	1 1/2 teaspoons
Bread flour	487g	3 3/4 cups, spooned and leveled
Instant yeast	—	2 teaspoons
Unsalted butter, cut into cubes, at room temperature	85g	6 tablespoons
Egg white or other crust-browning wash (optional; see page 26)	—	—

Hands-Off Method

In the order listed, add all the ingredients (except for the egg white) to the bread machine's baking pan. Program the machine to its **WHITE** setting and **MEDIUM** crust. Lock the pan into the machine, close the lid, and press **START**. If desired, after the loaf's final rise (usually around 1:30 from completion), pause the program and brush the proofed loaf with egg white. Once complete, remove the pan from the machine and let the bread cool in the pan for 10 to 15 minutes. Then tip the loaf out onto a cooling rack to cool completely before slicing.

continued →

Buttery Brioche
continued

Hand-Shaped Method

In the order listed, add all the ingredients (except for the egg white) to the bread machine's baking pan. Select **DOUGH**, lock the pan into the machine, close the lid, and press **START**. At the completion of the cycle, the dough should be doubled in size; if not, leave it in the machine for additional time as needed.

Transfer the dough to a clean work surface. If it's too sticky to handle, dust it lightly with flour; this is a wet dough, so you will likely need it, and use a bench scraper to help lift and move it around. Gently stretch it to a thickness of about 1 inch, then shape it to fit a 9 × 5-inch loaf pan (see page 30, for tips) if baking in a home oven.

Place the loaf seam-side down back in the bread machine pan (or in a greased loaf pan if baking in a home oven). Close the bread machine lid and proof in the bread machine (or cover the loaf pan with a clean towel or food wrap and proof in a warm spot in the kitchen) until doubled in size, about 1 hour. You can also proof the dough overnight in the refrigerator; allow it to warm up at room temperature for 30 to 60 minutes before baking.

To bake in a bread machine: If desired, brush the top of the proofed loaf with egg white and lock the pan into the bread machine. Select the **BAKE** setting and bake the loaf for 1 hour. Remove the pan from the machine and allow the bread to cool in the pan for 15 minutes. Then tip out onto a cooling rack to cool completely before slicing.

To bake in a home oven: Preheat the oven to 350°F, using convection if available. If desired, brush the top of the loaf with egg white, and score the bread by making a long slash down the length of the loaf with a sharp knife. Bake until browned and hollow-sounding when you tap on the loaf or an instant-read thermometer reads 190°F, 40 to 50 minutes. Cool in the pan for at least 15 minutes. Then tip out onto a cooling rack to cool completely before slicing.

Leftovers and Storage: Best eaten on the day it's made, but leftovers can be revived by toasting. Stored in an airtight bag or container, the sliced loaf can be frozen for up to 1 month.

Variations

Orange-Scented Brioche: Add 1 teaspoon orange blossom water and the grated zest of 1 orange to the wet ingredients.

Brioche Hamburger Buns: Shape into 8 or 10 buns, following the shaping, proofing, and baking instructions in Hamburger Buns (page 168).

Multigrain Loaf

Those with a soft spot for hippie-granola "health" cafés that serve sandwiches stuffed with things like mashed avocado, alfalfa sprouts, and honey-mustard dressing will recognize this bread. It's a little squatter than its white-flour counterparts, but just as much of a classic, with a sturdy, tight crumb and copious flecks of mixed grains and seeds throughout. This version is moist, lightly sweetened, and dense with nutrients.

Makes 1 loaf

Ingredient	Grams	Volume
Seed and Grain Soak		
Multigrain hot cereal mix	135g	3/4 cup
Raw sunflower seeds	40g	1/4 cup
Flaxseeds	22g	2 tablespoons
Boiling water	240g	1 cup
Dough		
Cool water	135g	1/2 cup plus 1 tablespoon
Maple syrup	60g	3 tablespoons
Fine sea salt	10g	1 1/2 teaspoons
Bread flour	325g	2 1/2 cups, spooned and leveled
Whole wheat flour or white whole wheat flour	105g	3/4 cup, spooned and leveled
Unsalted butter or vegan butter, cut into cubes, at room temperature	28g	2 tablespoons
Instant yeast	—	2 teaspoons
Egg white or other crust-browning wash (optional; see page 26)	—	—

continued →

Multigrain Loaf
continued

Make the seed and grain soak: In a small heatproof bowl, combine the cereal mix, seeds, and boiling water. Stir to combine, then allow the mixture to cool, 30 to 40 minutes.

Hands-Off Method

Scrape the soaked grains and seeds into the bread machine's baking pan. Add all remaining dough ingredients except for the egg white, in the order listed. Program the machine to its **MULTIGRAIN** or **WHOLE WHEAT** setting and **MEDIUM** or **DARK** crust. Lock the pan into the machine, close the lid, and press **START**. If desired, after the loaf's final rise (usually around 1:30 from completion), pause the program and brush the proofed loaf with egg white. Once complete, remove the bread from the machine and let cool in the pan for 10 to 15 minutes. Then tip the loaf out of the pan onto a cooling rack to cool completely before slicing.

Hand-Shaped Method

Scrape the soaked grains and seeds into the bread machine's baking pan. Add all remaining dough ingredients except for the egg white, in the order listed. Select **DOUGH**, lock the pan into the machine, close the lid, and press **START**. At the completion of the cycle, the dough should be doubled in size; if not, leave it in the machine for additional time as needed.

Transfer the dough to a clean work surface. If it's too sticky to handle, dust it lightly with flour, but resist adding any more than necessary, and use a bench scraper to help lift and move it around. Gently stretch it to a thickness of about 1 inch, then shape it to fit a 9 × 5-inch loaf pan (see page 30, for tips) if baking in a home oven.

Place the loaf seam-side down back in the bread machine pan (or in a greased loaf pan if baking in a home oven). Close the bread machine lid and proof in the bread machine (or cover the loaf pan with a clean towel or food wrap and proof in a warm spot in the kitchen) until doubled in size, about 1 hour.

To bake in a bread machine: If desired, brush the top of the proofed loaf with egg white and lock the pan into the bread machine. Select the **BAKE** setting and bake the loaf for 1 hour. Remove the pan from the machine and allow the bread to cool in the pan for 15 minutes. Then tip out onto a cooling rack to cool completely before slicing.

To bake in a home oven: Preheat the oven to 350°F, using convection if available. If desired, brush the top of the loaf with egg white, and score the bread by making a long slash down the length of the loaf with a sharp knife. Bake until browned and hollow-sounding when you tap on the loaf or an instant-read thermometer reads 190°F, 40 to 50 minutes. Cool in the pan for at least 15 minutes. Then tip out onto a cooling rack to cool completely before slicing.

Leftovers and Storage: Keeps for up to 3 days, wrapped loosely at room temperature. Stored in an airtight bag or container, the sliced loaf can be frozen for up to 1 month.

Simple Tender Yogurt Loaf

This easy loaf has a pleasant tang and a soft, tender interior that calls to mind Wonder bread—in such a good way. And unlike buttery enriched breads, the yogurt here yields a loaf that's light and has a longer shelf life. A sheep's milk, goat's milk, or your favorite plain nondairy yogurt can all be used, each adding its own character to the bread.

Makes 1 loaf

Ingredient	Grams	Volume
Plain yogurt	180g	3/4 cup
Tepid water	180g	3/4 cup
Honey	40g	2 tablespoons
Fine sea salt	10g	1 1/2 teaspoons
Bread flour	487g	3 3/4 cups, spooned and leveled
Unsalted butter or vegan butter, cut into cubes	28g	2 tablespoons
Instant yeast	—	2 teaspoons
Egg white or other crust-browning wash (optional; see page 26)	—	—

Hands-Off Method

In the order listed, add all the ingredients (except for the egg white) to the bread machine's baking pan. Program the machine to its **WHITE** setting and **MEDIUM** crust. Lock the pan into the machine, close the lid, and press **START**. If desired, after the loaf's final rise (usually around 1:30 from completion), pause the program and brush the proofed loaf with egg white. Once complete, remove the bread from the machine and let cool in the pan for 10 to 15 minutes. Then tip the loaf out of the pan onto a cooling rack to cool completely before slicing.

Hand-Shaped Method

In the order listed, add all the ingredients (except for the egg white) to the bread machine's baking pan. Select **DOUGH**, lock the pan into the machine, close the lid, and press **START**. At the completion of the cycle, the dough should be doubled in size; if not, leave it in the machine for additional time as needed.

continued →

Simple Tender Yogurt Loaf
continued

Transfer the dough to a clean work surface. If it's too sticky to handle, dust it lightly with flour, but resist adding any more than necessary, and use a bench scraper to help lift and move it around. Gently stretch it to a thickness of about 1 inch, then shape it to fit a 9 × 5-inch loaf pan (see page 30, for tips) if baking in a home oven.

Place the loaf seam-side down back in the bread machine pan (or in a greased loaf pan if baking in a home oven). Close the bread machine lid and proof in the bread machine (or cover the loaf pan with a clean towel or food wrap and proof in a warm spot in the kitchen) until doubled in size, about 1 hour.

You can also proof the dough overnight in the refrigerator; allow it to warm up at room temperature for 30 to 60 minutes before baking.

To bake in a bread machine: If desired, brush the top of the proofed loaf with egg white and lock the pan into the bread machine. Select the **BAKE** setting and bake the loaf for 1 hour. Remove the pan from the machine and allow the bread to cool in the pan for 15 minutes. Then tip out onto a cooling rack to cool completely before slicing.

To bake in a home oven: Preheat the oven to 350°F, using convection if available. If desired, brush the top of the loaf with egg white, and score the bread by making a long slash down the length of the loaf with a sharp knife. Bake until browned and hollow-sounding when you tap on the loaf or an instant-read thermometer reads 190°F, 40 to 50 minutes. Cool in the pan for at least 15 minutes. Then tip out onto a cooling rack to cool completely before slicing.

Leftovers and Storage: Keeps for up to 2 days, wrapped loosely at room temperature. Stored in an airtight bag or container, the sliced loaf can be frozen for up to 1 month.

Is Your Bread Machine Rattling Around?

Some bread machine models can rock and rattle so much as they knead that you might worry they'll catapult off your countertop. To prevent that from happening, fold a kitchen towel in half and lay it beneath the machine to help anchor it.

3

Special Occasion & Savory Breads

Breads with a premium on self-expression, with distinctive characteristics from specialty flours, flavorful additions, and less common techniques. Memorable snacks to nibble on through the day, these loaves are also unique additions to dinner spreads.

Honey-Barley Milk Bread

Milk bread, known as shokupan in Japan, is a fluffy, buttery enriched bread that employs a roux, or tangzhong, by which a portion of flour and liquid is cooked to a thick, pudding-like texture before going into the dough. This process sets the starches in the flour and imparts a soft, pillowy texture and extends the shelf life. Incorporating some barley flour, with its soft texture and nutty sweetness, flecks the baked loaf with bran and is my favorite riff on the classic style.

Makes 1 loaf

Ingredient	Grams	Volume
Roux		
Water	180g	3/4 cup
All-purpose flour or bread flour	45g	1/3 cup
Dough		
Whole milk	120g	1/2 cup
Eggs	100g	2 large
Honey	44g	1/4 cup
Fine sea salt	10g	1 1/2 teaspoons
Bread flour	325g	2 1/2 cups, spooned and leveled
Barley flour	120g	1 cup, spooned and leveled
Unsalted butter, at room temperature, cut into cubes	70g	5 tablespoons
Instant yeast	—	2 teaspoons
Egg white or other crust-browning wash (optional; see page 26)	—	—

continued →

Honey-Barley Milk Bread
continued

Make the roux: In a small saucepan, combine the water and all-purpose flour and whisk constantly over medium heat until the mixture thickens to the consistency of pudding, 3 to 5 minutes. Let cool.

Hands-Off Method

Scrape the cooled roux into the bread machine's baking pan. In the order listed, add all the dough ingredients (except for the egg white). Program the machine to its **WHITE** setting and **MEDIUM** crust. Lock the pan into the machine, close the lid, and press **START**. If desired, after the loaf's final rise (usually around 1:30 from completion), pause the program and brush the proofed loaf with egg white. Once complete, remove the bread from the machine and let cool in the pan for 10 to 15 minutes. Then tip the loaf out of the pan onto a cooling rack to cool completely before slicing.

Hand-Shaped Method

Scrape the cooled roux into the bread machine's baking pan. In the order listed, add all the dough ingredients (except for the egg white). Select **DOUGH**, lock the pan into the machine, close the lid, and press **START**. At the completion of the cycle, the dough should be doubled in size; if not, leave it in the machine for additional time as needed.

Transfer the dough to a clean work surface. It will be soft and not entirely smooth. If it's too sticky to handle, dust it lightly with flour, but resist adding any more than necessary, and use a bench scraper to help lift and move it around. Gently stretch it to a thickness of about 1 inch, then shape it to fit a 9 × 5-inch loaf pan (see page 30, for tips) if baking in a home oven.

Place the loaf seam-side down back in the bread machine pan (or in a greased loaf pan if baking in a home oven). Close the bread machine lid and proof in the bread machine (or cover the loaf pan with a clean towel or food wrap and proof in a warm spot in the kitchen) until doubled in size, about 1 hour. You can also proof the dough overnight in the refrigerator; allow it to warm up at room temperature for 30 to 60 minutes before baking.

To bake in a bread machine: If desired, brush the top of the proofed loaf with egg white and lock the pan into the bread machine. Select the **BAKE** setting and bake the loaf for 1 hour. Remove the pan from the machine and allow the bread to cool in the pan for 15 minutes. Then tip out onto a cooling rack to cool completely before slicing.

Variations

Classic Milk Bread: Replace barley flour with 130g (1 cup) bread flour.

Milk-Bread Hamburger Buns: Shape into 8 or 10 rolls, following the shaping, proofing, and baking instructions in Hamburger Buns (page 168).

To bake in a home oven: Preheat the oven to 350°F, using convection if available. If desired, brush the top of the loaf with egg white and score the bread by making a long slash down the length of the loaf with a sharp knife. Bake until browned and hollow-sounding when you tap on the loaf or an instant-read thermometer reads 190°F, 40 to 50 minutes. Cool in the pan for at least 15 minutes. Then tip out onto a cooling rack to cool completely before slicing.

Leftovers and Storage: Keeps for up to 3 days, wrapped loosely at room temperature. Stored in an airtight bag or container, the sliced loaf can be frozen for up to 1 month.

Tip: Let the Loaf Cool Before Slicing

It's so tempting to cut into a warm, fragrant loaf of bread as soon as it comes out of the oven—but if at all possible, wait at least 30 minutes. If you cut too soon, the crumb won't be set, and will have a gummy consistency. But if allowed to cool, the crumb will set properly and hold its shape.

Porridge Loaf with Flaxseeds

Any type of cooked, leftover oatmeal—even leftover polenta or grits—works well in this tender porridge loaf. Cooked steel-cut oats are my preference, adding barely discernible chew in addition to their milky sweetness. And similar to the effect of the cooked roux in the Honey-Barley Milk Bread (page 77), the cooked porridge extends the shelf life of the bread. It's a tall, soft loaf with a pretty open crumb.

Makes 1 loaf

Ingredient	Grams	Volume
Cooked steel-cut oats (see page 83), cooled	200g	3/4 cup
Tepid water	210g	3/4 cup plus 2 tablespoons
Brown sugar or coconut sugar	14g	1 tablespoon
Fine sea salt	10g	1 1/2 teaspoons
Bread flour	325g	2 1/2 cups, spooned and leveled
Whole wheat flour or white whole wheat flour	105g	3/4 cup, spooned and leveled
Unsalted butter or vegan butter, cut into cubes, at room temperature	28g	2 tablespoons
Flaxseeds, plus extra for sprinkling	22g	2 tablespoons
Instant yeast	—	2 teaspoons
Egg white or other crust-browning wash (optional; see page 26)	—	—

continued →

Porridge Loaf with Flaxseeds
continued

Hands-Off Method

In the order listed, add all the ingredients (except for the egg white) to the bread machine's baking pan. Program the machine to its **WHEAT** setting and **MEDIUM** or **DARK** crust. Lock the pan into the machine, close the lid, and press **START**. If desired, after the loaf's final rise (usually around 1:30 from completion), pause the program and brush the proofed loaf with egg white. Once complete, remove the bread from the machine and let cool in the pan for 10 to 15 minutes. Then tip the loaf out of the pan onto a cooling rack to cool completely before slicing.

Hand-Shaped Method

In the order listed, add all the ingredients (except for the egg white) to the bread machine's baking pan. Select **DOUGH**, lock the pan into the machine, close the lid, and press **START**. At the completion of the cycle, the dough should be doubled in size; if not, leave it in the machine for additional time as needed.

Transfer the dough to a clean work surface. If it's too sticky to handle, dust it lightly with flour, but resist adding any more than necessary, and use a bench scraper to help lift and move it around. Gently stretch it to a thickness of about 1 inch, then shape it to fit a 9 × 5-inch loaf pan (see page 30, for tips) if baking in a home oven.

Place the loaf seam-side down back in the bread machine pan (or in a greased loaf pan if baking in a home oven). Close the bread machine lid and proof in the bread machine (or cover the loaf pan with a clean towel or food wrap and proof in a warm spot in the kitchen) until doubled in size, about 1 hour. You can also proof the dough overnight in the refrigerator; allow it to warm up at room temperature for 30 to 60 minutes before baking.

To bake in a bread machine: If desired, brush the top of the proofed loaf with egg white, sprinkle with a few pinches of flaxseeds, and lock the pan into the bread machine. Select the **BAKE** setting and bake the loaf for 1 hour. Remove the pan from the machine and allow the bread to cool in the pan for 15 minutes. Then tip out onto a cooling rack to cool completely before slicing.

To bake in a home oven: Preheat the oven to 350°F, using convection if available. If desired, brush the top of the loaf with egg white, sprinkle with a few pinches of flaxseeds, and score the bread by making a long slash down the length of the loaf with a sharp knife. Bake until browned and hollow-sounding when you tap on the loaf or an instant-read thermometer reads 190°F, 40 to 50 minutes. Cool in the pan for at least 15 minutes. Then tip out onto a cooling rack to cool completely before slicing.

Leftovers and Storage: Keeps for up to 3 days, wrapped loosely at room temperature. Stored in an airtight bag or container, the sliced loaf can be frozen for up to 1 month.

How to Cook Steel-Cut Oats

In a saucepan, melt about **1 tablespoon butter** over medium heat. Stir in **1 cup steel-cut oats** and toast, swirling or stirring the pan often, until fragrant, 2 to 3 minutes. Add **3 cups water, 1 cup milk,** and **1/2 teaspoon salt.** Bring to a boil. Stir, reduce to a simmer, partially cover, and simmer gently until thickened to your liking, 15 to 20 minutes. *Makes 4 cups (960g)*

Burnt Honey–Cumin Spelt Loaf

Inspired by an incredible sourdough loaf that I had at Goodwood Bake Shop in Sydney, Australia, the scent of a combination of honey, heated just to the smoking point to take on a slight edge of bitterness, and the wildly aromatic cumin seeds is impossible to forget. This loaf benefits from a longer, slower rise, if you have time (see page 24, for tips).

Makes 1 loaf

Ingredient	Grams	Volume
Burnt Honey		
Honey	100g	5 tablespoons
Tepid water	60g	1/4 cup
Dough		
Tepid water	300g	1 1/4 cups
Fine sea salt	10g	1 1/2 teaspoons
Bread flour	325g	2 1/2 cups, spooned and leveled
Spelt flour	245g	1 3/4 cups, spooned and leveled
Cumin seeds, toasted and lightly crushed or left whole	8g	1 tablespoon
Unsalted butter or vegan butter, cut into cubes, at room temperature	28g	2 tablespoons
Instant yeast	—	2 teaspoons
Egg white or other crust-browning wash (optional; see page 26)	—	—

continued →

Burnt Honey–Cumin Spelt Loaf
continued

Make the burnt honey:
In a small saucepan, bring the honey to a simmer over medium heat, swirling the pan or whisking periodically. Cook until the surface foam darkens to a reddish-brown color and the first wisp of smoke appears, 5 to 10 minutes. Remove from the heat and, using caution since the mixture will bubble up, whisk in the water. Allow to cool.

Hands-Off Method
Add the cooled honey mixture to the bread machine's baking pan. In the order listed, add all the dough ingredients (except for the egg white). Program the machine to its **WHEAT** setting and **MEDIUM** crust. Lock the pan into the machine, close the lid, and press **START**. If desired, after the loaf's final rise (usually around 1:30 from completion), pause the program and brush the proofed loaf with egg white. Once complete, remove the bread from the machine and let cool in the pan for 10 to 15 minutes. Then tip the loaf out of the pan onto a cooling rack to cool completely before slicing.

Hand-Shaped Method
Add the cooled honey mixture to the bread machine's baking pan. In the order listed, add all the dough ingredients (except for the egg white). Select **DOUGH**, lock the pan into the machine, close the lid, and press **START**. At the completion of the cycle, the dough should be doubled in size; if not, leave it in the machine for additional time as needed.

Transfer the dough to a clean work surface. If it's too sticky to handle, dust it lightly with flour, but resist adding any more than necessary, and use a bench scraper to help lift and move it around. Gently stretch it to a thickness of about 1 inch, then shape it to fit a 9 × 5-inch loaf pan (see page 30, for tips) if baking in a home oven.

Place the loaf seam-side down back in the bread machine pan (or in a greased loaf pan if baking in a home oven). Close the bread machine lid and proof in the bread machine (or cover the loaf pan with a clean towel or food wrap and proof in a warm spot in the kitchen) until doubled in size, about 1 hour. You can also proof the dough overnight in the refrigerator; allow it to warm up at room temperature for 30 to 60 minutes before baking.

To bake in a bread machine:
If desired, brush the top of the proofed loaf with egg white, and lock the pan into the bread machine. Select the **BAKE** setting and bake the loaf for 1 hour. Remove the pan from the machine and allow the bread to cool in the pan for 15 minutes. Then tip out onto a cooling rack to cool completely before slicing.

To bake in a home oven:
Preheat the oven to 350°F, using convection if available. If desired, brush the top of the loaf with egg white, and score the bread by making a long slash down the length of the loaf with a sharp knife. Bake until browned and hollow-sounding when you tap on the loaf or an instant-read thermometer reads 190°F, 40 to 50 minutes. Cool in the pan for at least 15 minutes. Then tip out onto a cooling rack to cool completely before slicing.

Leftovers and Storage: Keeps for up to 2 days, wrapped loosely at room temperature. Stored in an airtight bag or container, the sliced loaf can be frozen for up to 1 month.

Irish Brown Bread

Irish brown bread, like soda bread, isn't leavened with yeast, so it requires some slight tinkering of the bread machine to customize a program. Overmixing will toughen the crumb, so you'll need to use the mixing function just until the dough is combined, and then switch to the bake function. But your oversight will be rewarded with a dense, craggy, sustaining loaf full of hearty ingredients and malty flavor. Be sure to have good butter on hand.

Makes 1 loaf

Ingredient	Grams	Volume
Stout beer	330g	1 (11- or 12-ounce) bottle
Plain yogurt or buttermilk	60g	1/4 cup
Unsalted butter or vegan butter, melted	42g	3 tablespoons
Brown sugar	50g	1/4 cup
Molasses	42g	2 tablespoons
Baking soda	10g	2 teaspoons
Fine sea salt	10g	1 1/2 teaspoons
Whole wheat flour or white whole wheat flour	420g	3 cups, spooned and leveled

In the order listed, add all ingredients to the bread machine's baking pan. Select **DOUGH**, or create a custom setting to **KNEAD** the mixture for 5 minutes. Lock the pan into the machine, close the lid, and press **START**. Watching closely, as soon as the mixture is combined, halt the program and turn off the machine (this will only take a few minutes; you can also mix the dough by hand to prevent overmixing). Use a flexible spatula to tidy up the edges and smooth the top.

Program a **BAKE** setting for 1:10 and press **START**. Once the cycle is complete, remove the bread from the machine

continued →

Irish Brown Bread
continued

and let cool in the pan for 10 to 15 minutes. Then tip the loaf out of the pan onto a cooling rack to cool for at least 15 minutes before slicing.

Leftovers and Storage: Keeps for up to 2 days, wrapped loosely at room temperature. Stored in an airtight bag or container, the sliced loaf can be frozen for up to 1 month.

Variation

Vegan Irish Brown Bread: Use plain nondairy yogurt, or make vegan buttermilk by pouring 1 teaspoon apple cider vinegar into a measuring glass and topping it off with enough plant-based milk to measure ¼ cup.

Nut & Seed Loaf

This squat, dense gluten-free loaf is an adaptation of "Stone Age" or "Paleo" bread, both of which have vaguely Nordic origins. It's typically bound with whole eggs (or in vegan adaptations, with psyllium husk), but I prefer egg whites, which work well to both bind and add extra protein. Since there's no kneading, this loaf is easy to make without a bread machine, but the machine's enclosed chamber is handy for the long hydration time, and its relatively low baking temperature is ideal for achieving the right texture. Similar to Irish Brown Bread (page 87), you'll need to do some slight overwriting of the machine's presets.

Makes 1 squat loaf

Ingredient	Grams	Volume
Tepid water	240g	1 cup
Liquid egg whites (about 4 egg whites) or 3 eggs	120g	1/2 cup
Extra-virgin olive oil	44g	1/4 cup
Maple syrup	21g	1 tablespoon
Fine sea salt	10g	1 1/2 teaspoons
Old-fashioned rolled oats	120g	1 cup
Sunflower seeds or pumpkin seeds, or a combination	150g	1 cup
Whole almonds, hazelnuts, or walnuts (unroasted)	70g	1/2 cup
Flaxseed meal	60g	1/2 cup
Almond flour	50g	1/2 cup
Chia seeds	25g	2 tablespoons

continued →

Nut & Seed Loaf
continued

In the order listed, add all the ingredients to the bread machine's baking pan. Select **DOUGH**, or create a custom setting to **KNEAD** the mixture for 5 minutes. Lock the pan into the machine, close the lid, and press **START**. Once the mixture is combined, after about 5 minutes, halt the program and turn off the machine. Use a flexible spatula to tidy up the edges of the pan and smooth the top.

Leave the dough to hydrate for at least 4 hours and up to 12 hours. (I leave mine in the machine at room temperature, but the pan can also be covered with food wrap and transferred to the refrigerator; it can be baked directly out of the fridge, no need to bring it to room temperature first.)

Lock the pan back in the bread machine, close the lid, and program it to **BAKE** for 1:20, then press **START**. Once the cycle is complete, remove the bread from the machine and allow it to cool completely in the pan before removing. This bread is best served sliced thinly and toasted.

Leftovers and Storage: Keeps for up to 1 week in an airtight container in the refrigerator. Stored in an airtight bag or container, the sliced loaf can be frozen for up to 1 month.

Variation

Vegan Nut & Seed Loaf: Replace the egg and tepid water with 1 tablespoon psyllium husk powder whisked into 1½ cups water.

Scallion Cheddar Loaf

This bread's incredibly tender, brioche-like softness is only enhanced by its decadently comforting flavor profile. It warms your kitchen with the intoxicating aromas of cheese and alliums, and it's the type of bread that I reach for to accompany soups, stew, and chili on cool fall and winter days. Leftovers are excellent in a breakfast strata (see Overnight Breakfast Strata, page 198).

Makes 1 loaf

Ingredient	Grams	Volume
Tepid water	120g	3/4 cup
Whole milk	80g	1/3 cup
Egg	50g	1 large
Runny honey	20g	1 tablespoon
Fine sea salt	7g	1 teaspoon
Bread flour	490g	3 3/4 cups, spooned and leveled
Coarsely ground black pepper	—	1/2 teaspoon
Garlic powder	—	1 teaspoon
Grated cheddar cheese, plus more for sprinkling	75g	1 cup
Scallions, thinly sliced (3 to 4)	75g	1 cup
Unsalted butter, cut into cubes, at room temperature	42g	3 tablespoons
Instant yeast	—	2 teaspoons
Egg white or other crust-browning wash (optional; see page 26)	—	—

continued →

Scallion Cheddar Loaf
continued

Hands-Off Method

In the order listed, add all the ingredients (except for the egg white) to the bread machine's baking pan. Program the machine to its **WHITE** setting and **MEDIUM** crust. Lock the pan into the machine, close the lid, and press **START**. If desired, after the loaf's final rise (usually around 1:30 from completion), pause the program and brush the proofed loaf with egg white and sprinkle with additional cheese. Once complete, remove the bread from the machine and let cool in the pan for 10 to 15 minutes. Then tip the loaf out of the pan onto a cooling rack to cool completely before slicing.

Hand-Shaped Method

In the order listed, add all the ingredients (except for the egg white) to the bread machine's baking pan. Select **DOUGH**, lock the pan into the machine, close the lid, and press **START**. At the completion of the cycle, the dough should be doubled in size; if not, leave it in the machine for additional time as needed.

Transfer the dough to a clean work surface. If it's too sticky to handle, dust it lightly with flour, but resist adding any more than necessary, and use a bench scraper to help lift and move it around. Gently stretch it to a thickness of about 1 inch, then shape it to fit a 9 × 5-inch loaf pan (see page 30, for tips) if baking in a home oven.

Place the loaf seam-side down back in the bread machine pan (or in a greased loaf pan if baking in a home oven). Close the bread machine lid and proof in the bread machine (or cover the loaf pan with a clean towel or food wrap and proof in a warm spot in the kitchen) until doubled in size, about 1 hour. You can also proof the dough overnight in the refrigerator; allow it to warm up at room temperature for 30 to 60 minutes before baking.

To bake in a bread machine: If desired, brush the top of the proofed loaf with egg white and sprinkle with additional cheddar. Lock the pan into the bread machine. Select the **BAKE** setting and bake the loaf for 1 hour. Remove the pan from the machine and allow the bread to cool in the pan for 15 minutes. Then tip out onto a cooling rack to cool for at least 15 minutes before slicing.

To bake in a home oven: Preheat the oven to 350°F, using convection if available. If desired, brush the top of the loaf with egg white and sprinkle with additional cheddar, and score the bread by making a long slash down the length of the loaf with a sharp knife. Bake until browned and hollow-sounding when you tap on the loaf or an instant-read thermometer reads 190°F, 40 to 50 minutes. Cool in the pan for at least 15 minutes. Then tip out onto a cooling rack to cool for at least 15 minutes before slicing.

Leftovers and Storage: Keeps for up to 2 days, wrapped loosely at room temperature. Stored in an airtight bag or container, the sliced loaf can be frozen for up to 1 month.

Plush Tofu Protein Loaf

Inspired by various types of protein bread that are amped up with cottage cheese and/or egg whites, this higher-protein-than-typical bread instead employs silken tofu, which blends seamlessly into the dough while it kneads in the bread machine. If you aren't yet a fan of tofu, I encourage you to still give this loaf a try anyway—rather than lend a lot of flavor, the tofu makes the bread appealingly squishy and satisfyingly rich.

Makes 1 loaf

Ingredient	Grams	Volume
Silken tofu (1 package)	350g	12 ounces
Egg	50g	1 large
Maple syrup	40g	2 tablespoons
Avocado oil or extra-virgin olive oil	11g	1 tablespoon
Fine sea salt	10g	1½ teaspoons
Bread flour	470g	3½ cups plus 2 tablespoons, spooned and leveled
Instant yeast	—	2 teaspoons
Egg white or other crust-browning wash (optional; see page 26)	—	—

Hands-Off Method

In the order listed, add all the ingredients (except for the egg white) to the bread machine's baking pan. Program the machine to its **WHITE** setting and **MEDIUM** crust. Lock the pan into the machine, close the lid, and press **START**. If desired, after the loaf's final rise (usually around 1:30 from completion), pause the program and brush the proofed loaf with egg white. Once complete, remove the bread from the machine and let cool in the pan for 10 to 15 minutes. Then tip the loaf out of the pan onto a cooling rack to cool completely before slicing.

Hand-Shaped Method

In the order listed, add all the ingredients (except for the egg white) to the bread machine's baking pan. Select **DOUGH**, lock the pan into the machine, close the lid, and press **START**. At the completion of the cycle,

continued →

UNBLEACHED
WHEAT
ORGANIC SIFTED ALL-PURPOSE FLOUR
MAINE GRAINS.

Plush Tofu Protein Loaf

continued

the dough should be doubled in size; if not, leave it in the machine for additional time as needed.

Transfer the dough to a clean work surface. If it's too sticky to handle, dust it lightly with flour, but resist adding any more than necessary, and use a bench scraper to help lift and move it around. Gently stretch it to a thickness of about 1 inch, then shape it to fit a 9 × 5-inch loaf pan (see page 30, for tips) if baking in a home oven.

Place the loaf seam-side down back in the bread machine pan (or in a greased loaf pan if baking in a home oven). Close the bread machine lid and proof in the bread machine (or cover the loaf pan with a clean towel or food wrap and proof in a warm spot in the kitchen) until doubled in size, about 1 hour. You can also proof the dough overnight in the refrigerator; allow it to warm up at room temperature for 30 to 60 minutes before baking.

To bake in a bread machine: If desired, brush the top of the proofed loaf with egg white and lock the pan into the bread machine. Select the **BAKE** setting and bake the loaf for 1 hour. Remove the pan from the machine and allow the bread to cool in the pan for 15 minutes. Then tip out onto a cooling rack to cool completely before slicing.

To bake in a home oven: Preheat the oven to 350°F, using convection if available. If desired, brush the top of the loaf with egg white and score the bread by making a long slash down the length of the loaf with a sharp knife. Bake until browned and hollow-sounding when you tap on the loaf or an instant-read thermometer reads 190°F, 40 to 50 minutes. Cool in the pan for at least 15 minutes. Then tip out onto a cooling rack to cool completely before slicing.

Leftovers and Storage: Keeps for up to 2 days, wrapped loosely at room temperature. Stored in an airtight bag or container, the sliced loaf can be frozen for up to 1 month.

Variation

Vegan Tofu Protein Loaf: Replace the egg with 3 tablespoons water and 2 teaspoons additional avocado oil. Watch as the dough kneads, and add an additional 1 to 2 tablespoons of flour if it is too wet.

4

Spiced & Sweet

Vibrant accent breads with sweeter and spice-forward flavor profiles—perfect for brunches and festive breakfasts. They also play contrasting roles to savory sandwich fillings and rich seasonal menus.

Cardamom-Spiced Monkey Bread

Squarely in the "sticky bun" family of sweet breads, Monkey Bread is a thrill because the only reasonable way to eat it is to pry it apart with your fingers. This recipe incorporates a bit of whole wheat into the dough and opts for cardamom, rather than cinnamon, as the lead spice, taking inspiration from Swedish cardamom knots known as *kardemummabullar*.

Makes 1 loaf

Ingredient	Grams	Volume
Dough		
Whole milk	180g	3/4 cup
Eggs	100g	2 large
Sugar	55g	1/4 cup
Fine sea salt	10g	1 1/2 teaspoons
Bread flour	325g	2 1/2 cups, spooned and leveled
Whole wheat pastry flour or whole wheat flour	175g	1 1/4 cups, spooned and leveled
Instant yeast	—	2 teaspoons
Unsalted butter, cut into 1/2-inch cubes, at room temperature	56g	4 tablespoons
Cardamom Coating		
Unsalted butter, melted	56g	4 tablespoons
Sugar	110g	1/2 cup
Ground cardamom (see Note)	—	1 tablespoon

continued →

Cardamom-Spiced Monkey Bread
continued

Vanilla Caramel Sauce		
Unsalted butter, melted	56g	4 tablespoons
Sugar	28g	2 tablespoons
Honey	40g	2 tablespoons
Vanilla extract	—	1 teaspoon
Fine sea salt	—	1/4 teaspoon

Make the dough: In the order listed, add all the ingredients to the bread machine's baking pan. Select **DOUGH**, lock the pan into the machine, close the lid, and press **START**. At the completion of the cycle, the dough should be doubled in size; if not, leave it in the machine for additional time as needed.

Transfer the dough to a clean work surface. If it's too sticky to handle, dust it lightly with flour, but resist adding any more than necessary, and use a bench scraper to help lift and move it around. Divide into 30 equal portions and roll each one into a ball the size of a Ping-Pong ball.

For the cardamom coating: Put the melted butter in a shallow bowl. In a separate bowl, combine the sugar and cardamom. Working quickly one by one, roll each ball in butter, then in the cardamom/sugar mixture and pile them evenly into either the bread machine baking pan or a greased 9 × 5-inch loaf pan.

Close the bread machine lid and proof in the bread machine (or cover the loaf pan with a clean towel or food wrap and proof in a warm spot in the kitchen) until doubled in size, about 1 hour. You can also proof the dough overnight in the refrigerator; allow it to warm up at room temperature for 30 to 60 minutes before baking.

Meanwhile, make the vanilla caramel sauce: In a small saucepan, combine the butter, sugar, honey, vanilla, and salt and bring to a simmer, stirring often, until the sugar is melted. Remove from the heat and allow it to cool.

To bake in a bread machine: Pour the cooled caramel sauce evenly over the dough. Lock your pan into the bread machine. Select the **BAKE** setting and bake the loaf for 1 hour. Remove the pan from the machine and let it cool in the pan for 10 minutes. Then tip out onto a serving platter or cooling rack set on top of a sheet pan, to collect any syrupy drippings. Cool for 10 minutes more before serving warm.

To bake in a home oven: Preheat the oven to 350°F. Pour the cooled caramel sauce evenly over the dough. Bake until golden brown on the top, 40 to 50 minutes. Cool in the pan for at least 10 minutes. Then tip out onto a serving platter or cooling rack set on top of a sheet pan, to collect any syrupy drippings. Cool for 10 minutes more before serving warm.

Leftovers and Storage: Best on the day it's made, but the bread can be shaped and assembled, then baked off the next morning. Wrap leftovers in foil and reheat them in a 300°F oven for 10 to 15 minutes.

Note: For the most pronounced flavor, seek out whole cardamom seeds (either purchased in a jar as "whole cardamom seeds," or still in their pods, which are easy to crack open to dislodge the seeds) and freshly grind them in a mortar or with an electric spice grinder.

Variation

Classic Monkey Bread: Substitute ground cinnamon for the cardamom.

Golden Turmeric Honey Loaf

Vibrantly golden and flecked with black pepper, this is a soft loaf inspired by Indian turmeric tea—a warming, milky, medicinal beverage that I like best sweetened with honey. Enjoy the bread on its own, or use it for head-turning sandwiches and toasts, where it pairs nicely with everything from Thanksgiving leftovers to yogurt topped with sliced, salted cucumbers.

Makes 1 loaf

Ingredient	Grams	Volume
Whole milk or plant-based milk	360g	1½ cups
Honey	50g	2½ tablespoons
Fine sea salt	10g	1½ teaspoons
Bread flour	480g	3⅓ cups, spooned and leveled
Ground turmeric	10g	1 tablespoon
Finely ground black pepper	—	¼ teaspoon
Unsalted butter or vegan butter, cut into cubes, at room temperature	42g	3 tablespoons
Instant yeast	—	2 teaspoons
Egg white or other crust-browning wash (optional; see page 26)	—	—

Hands-Off Method

In the order listed, add all the ingredients (except for the egg white) to the bread machine's baking pan. Program the machine to its **WHITE** setting and **MEDIUM** crust. Lock the pan into the machine, close the lid, and press **START**. If desired, after the loaf's final rise (usually around 1:30 from completion), pause the program and brush the proofed loaf with egg white. Once complete, remove the bread from the machine and let cool in the pan for 10 to 15 minutes. Then tip the loaf out of the pan onto a cooling rack to cool completely before slicing.

continued →

Golden Turmeric Honey Loaf
continued

Hand-Shaped Method

In the order listed, add all the ingredients (except for the egg white) to the bread machine's baking pan. Select **DOUGH**, lock the pan into the machine, close the lid, and press **START**. At the completion of the cycle, the dough should be doubled in size; if not, leave it in the machine for additional time as needed.

Transfer the dough to a clean work surface. If it's too sticky to handle, dust it lightly with flour, but resist adding any more than necessary, and use a bench scraper to help lift and move it around. Gently stretch it to a thickness of about 1 inch, then shape it to fit a 9 × 5-inch loaf pan (see page 30, for tips) if baking in a home oven.

Place the loaf seam-side down back in the bread machine pan (or in a greased loaf pan if baking in a home oven). Close the bread machine lid and proof in the bread machine (or cover the loaf pan with a clean towel or food wrap and proof in a warm spot in the kitchen) until doubled in size, about 1 hour. You can also proof the dough overnight in the refrigerator; allow it to warm up at room temperature for 30 to 60 minutes before baking.

To bake in a bread machine: If desired, brush the top of the proofed loaf with egg white, and lock the pan into the bread machine. Select the **BAKE** setting and bake the loaf for 1 hour. Remove the pan from the machine and allow the bread to cool in the pan for 15 minutes. Then tip out onto a cooling rack to cool completely before slicing.

To bake in a home oven: Preheat the oven to 350°F, using convection if available. If desired, brush the top of the loaf with egg white and score the bread by making a long slash down the length of the loaf with a sharp knife. Bake until browned and hollow-sounding when you tap on the loaf or an instant-read thermometer reads 190°F, 40 to 50 minutes. Cool in the pan for at least 15 minutes. Then tip out onto a cooling rack to cool completely before slicing.

Leftovers and Storage: Keeps for up to 2 days, wrapped loosely at room temperature. Stored in an airtight bag or container, the sliced loaf can be frozen for up to 1 month.

Variation

Golden Turmeric Dinner Rolls: Divide the dough into 15 equal portions and follow the shaping, proofing, and baking instructions in Ranch Rolls (page 163).

Granola Loaf

This wheat- and oat-based dough, fragrant with coconut and a touch of cinnamon, is filled with nubby clusters of sweetness courtesy of a hefty dose of your favorite granola. It's perfect at breakfast and beloved by kids.

Makes 1 loaf

Ingredient	Grams	Volume
Granola Soak		
Your favorite granola (see Note)	110g	About 1½ cups
Whole milk or plant-based milk	30g	2 tablespoons
Dough		
Whole milk or plant-based milk	180g	¾ cup
Cool water	120g	¾ cup
Coconut sugar or brown sugar	55g	¼ cup
Coconut oil (melted or solid) or soft unsalted butter	28g	2 tablespoons
Fine sea salt	10g	1½ teaspoons
Bread flour	260g	2 cups, spooned and leveled
Whole wheat or white whole wheat flour	105g	¾ cup, spooned and leveled
Rolled oats, quick-cooking or old-fashioned	75g	¾ cup
Ground cinnamon	4g	1½ teaspoons
Instant yeast	—	2 teaspoons
Egg white or other crust-browning wash (optional; see page 26)	—	—

continued →

Granola Loaf
continued

Make the granola soak: In a small bowl, combine the granola with the milk.

Hands-Off Method

In the order listed, add all the dough ingredients (except for the egg white) to the bread machine's baking pan. Program the machine to its WHITE setting and MEDIUM crust. Lock the pan into the machine, close the lid, and press START.

When the alert for additions sounds off, scrape the soaked granola into the bread machine.

If desired, after the loaf's final rise (usually around 1:30 from completion), pause the program and brush the proofed loaf with egg white. Once the baking cycle is complete, remove the bread from the machine and let cool in the pan for 10 to 15 minutes. Then tip the loaf out of the pan onto a cooling rack to cool completely before slicing.

Hand-Shaped Method

In the order listed, add all the dough ingredients (except for the egg white) to the bread machine's baking pan. Select DOUGH, lock the pan into the machine, close the lid, and press START. At the completion of the cycle, the dough should be doubled in size; if not, leave it in the machine for additional time as needed.

Transfer the dough to a clean work surface. If it's too sticky to handle, dust it lightly with flour, but resist adding any more than necessary, and use a bench scraper to help lift and move it around. Gently stretch the dough to a thickness of about 1 inch, scatter about one-third of the soaked granola over the dough, then roll it up. Repeat this process twice more, until all of the granola is incorporated. (Alternatively, add it when the alert for additions sounds during the kneading stage.) Shape it to fit a 9 × 5-inch loaf pan (see page 30, for tips) if baking in a home oven.

Place the loaf seam-side down back in the bread machine pan (or in a greased loaf pan if baking in a home oven). Close the bread machine lid and proof in the bread machine (or cover the loaf pan with a clean towel or food wrap and proof in a warm spot in the kitchen) until doubled in size, about 1 hour. You can also proof the dough overnight in the refrigerator; allow it to warm up at room temperature for 30 to 60 minutes before baking.

To bake in a bread machine: If desired, brush the top of the proofed loaf with egg white and lock the pan into the bread machine. Select the BAKE setting and bake the loaf for 1 hour. Remove the pan from the machine and allow the bread to cool in the pan for 15 minutes. Then tip out onto a cooling rack to cool completely before slicing.

To bake in a home oven: Preheat the oven to 350°F, using convection if available. If desired, brush the top of the loaf with egg white, and score the bread by making a long slash down the length of the loaf with a sharp knife. Bake until browned and hollow-sounding when you tap on the loaf or an instant-read thermometer reads 190°F, 40 to 50 minutes. Cool in the pan for at least 15 minutes. Then tip out onto a cooling rack to cool completely before slicing.

Leftovers and Storage: Keeps for up to 2 days, wrapped loosely at room temperature. Stored in an airtight bag or container, the sliced loaf can be frozen for up to 1 month.

Maple Cornbread Loaf

There's something exciting about a cornbread that can be crumbled over a bowl of chili *or* sliced up loaf-style and used for sandwiches. This is lightly sweet and sunny in flavor, a perfect foil for bold flavors and rich sandwich fillings. I like to use a finely ground cornmeal because it integrates more seamlessly than a coarse, stone-ground one, lending flavor more than texture.

Makes 1 loaf

Ingredient	Grams	Volume
Whole milk or plant-based milk	180g	3/4 cup
Tepid water	80g	1/3 cup
Maple syrup	80g	1/4 cup
Fine sea salt	10g	1 1/2 teaspoons
Bread flour	357g	2 3/4 cups, spooned and leveled
Fine-grind cornmeal	150g	1 cup
Unsalted butter or vegan butter, cut into cubes, at room temperature	56g	4 tablespoons
Instant yeast	—	2 teaspoons
Egg white or other crust-browning wash (optional; see page 26)	—	—

Hands-Off Method

In the order listed, add all the ingredients (except for the egg white) to the bread machine's baking pan. Program the machine to its **WHEAT** setting and **MEDIUM** or **DARK** crust. Lock the pan into the machine, close the lid, and press **START**. If desired, after the loaf's final rise (usually around 1:30 from completion), pause the program and brush the proofed loaf with egg white. Once complete, remove the bread from the machine and let cool in the pan for 10 to 15 minutes. Then tip the loaf out of the pan onto a cooling rack to cool completely before slicing.

Hand-Shaped Method

In the order listed, add all the ingredients (except for the egg white) to the bread machine's baking pan. Select **DOUGH**, lock the pan into the machine, close the lid, and press **START**. At the completion of the cycle,

continued →

Maple Cornbread Loaf
continued

the dough should be doubled in size; if not, leave it in the machine for additional time as needed.

Transfer the dough to a clean work surface. If it's too sticky to handle, dust it lightly with flour, but resist adding any more than necessary, and use a bench scraper to help lift and move it around. Gently stretch it to a thickness of about 1 inch, then shape it to fit a 9 × 5-inch loaf pan (see page 30, for tips) if baking in a home oven.

Place the loaf seam-side down back in the bread machine pan (or in a greased loaf pan if baking in a home oven). Close the bread machine lid and proof in the bread machine (or cover the loaf pan with a clean towel or food wrap and proof in a warm spot in the kitchen) until doubled in size, about 1 hour. You can also proof the dough overnight in the refrigerator; allow it to warm up at room temperature for 30 to 60 minutes before baking.

To bake in a bread machine: If desired, brush the top of the proofed loaf with egg white, and lock the pan into the bread machine. Select the **BAKE** setting and bake the loaf for 1 hour. Remove the pan from the machine and allow the bread to cool in the pan for 15 minutes. Then tip out onto a cooling rack to cool completely before slicing.

To bake in a home oven: Preheat the oven to 350°F, using convection if available. If desired, brush the top of the loaf with egg white and score the bread by making a long slash down the length of the loaf with a sharp knife. Bake until browned and hollow-sounding when you tap on the loaf or an instant-read thermometer reads 190°F, 40 to 50 minutes. Cool in the pan for at least 15 minutes. Then tip out onto a cooling rack to cool completely before slicing.

Leftovers and Storage: Keeps for up to 2 days, wrapped loosely at room temperature. Stored in an airtight bag or container, the sliced loaf can be frozen for up to 1 month.

Variation

Green Chile Cornbread: **Add 1 (4-ounce) can diced green chiles, drained, when the alert for additions sounds off during the knead cycle.**

Spiced Squash Loaf

While inspired by the pumpkin “bread” that’s really more of a delicious loaf cake, this is a light, true-to-form bread infused with the same seasonal sweetness and classic spices. You’ll need exactly half of a 14.5-ounce can of pumpkin or squash puree (freeze the rest for the next time you make this recipe). It’s an excellent bread for a grilled cheese sandwich, with caramelized onions or fig jam tucked inside.

Makes 1 loaf

Ingredient	Grams	Volume
Butternut squash or pumpkin puree	212g	3/4 cup plus 1 tablespoon
Whole milk or plant-based milk	80g	1/2 cup
Egg	50g	1 large
Brown sugar	55g	1/4 cup
Fine sea salt	10g	1 1/2 teaspoons
Bread flour	423g	3 1/4 cups, spooned and leveled
Ground cinnamon	—	1 1/2 teaspoons
Freshly grated or ground nutmeg	—	1/2 teaspoon
Ground cloves	—	1/4 teaspoon
Unsalted butter, cut into cubes, at room temperature, or coconut oil	42g	3 tablespoons
Instant yeast	—	2 teaspoons
Egg white or other crust-browning wash (optional; see page 26)	—	—

continued →

Spiced Squash Loaf
continued

Hands-Off Method

In the order listed, add all the ingredients (except for the egg white) to the bread machine's baking pan. Program the machine to its **WHITE** setting and **MEDIUM** crust. Lock the pan into the machine, close the lid, and press **START**. If desired, after the loaf's final rise (usually around 1:30 from completion), pause the program and brush the proofed loaf with egg white. Once complete, remove the bread from the machine and let cool in the pan for 10 to 15 minutes. Then tip the loaf out of the pan onto a cooling rack to cool completely before slicing.

Hand-Shaped Method

In the order listed, add all the ingredients (except for the egg white) to the bread machine's baking pan. Select **DOUGH**, lock the pan into the machine, close the lid, and press **START**. At the completion of the cycle, the dough should be doubled in size; if not, leave it in the machine for additional time as needed.

Transfer the dough to a clean work surface. If it's too sticky to handle, dust it lightly with flour, but resist adding any more than necessary, and use a bench scraper to help lift and move it around. Gently stretch it to a thickness of about 1 inch, then shape it to fit a 9 × 5-inch loaf pan (see page 30, for tips) if baking in a home oven.

Place the loaf seam-side down back in the bread machine pan (or in a greased loaf pan if baking in a home oven). Close the bread machine lid and proof in the bread machine (or cover the loaf pan with a clean towel or food wrap and proof in a warm spot in the kitchen) until doubled in size, about 1 hour. You can also proof the dough overnight in the refrigerator; allow it to warm up at room temperature for 30 to 60 minutes before baking.

To bake in a bread machine: If desired, brush the top of the proofed loaf with egg white, and lock the pan into the bread machine. Select the **BAKE** setting and bake the loaf for 1 hour. Remove the pan from the machine and allow the bread to cool in the pan for 15 minutes. Then tip out onto a cooling rack to cool completely before slicing.

To bake in a home oven: Preheat the oven to 350°F, using convection if available. If desired, brush the top of the loaf with egg white and score the bread by making a long slash down the length of the loaf with a sharp knife. Bake until browned and hollow-sounding when you tap on the loaf or an instant-read thermometer reads 190°F, 40 to 50 minutes. Cool in the pan for at least 15 minutes. Then tip out onto a cooling rack to cool completely before slicing.

Leftovers and Storage: Keeps well for 2 days, loosely wrapped at room temperature. The sliced loaf can be frozen for up to 1 month.

Variations

Spiced Squash Loaf with Mix-Ins: Add 115g (3/4 cup) pumpkin seeds, 75g (1/2 cup) dried cherries or cranberries, or 150g (1 cup) dark chocolate chips or chunks at the alert during the knead cycle.

Soft Poppy Seed Loaf

A poppy seed muffin but in bread form, this loaf is tall and super soft, its light crumb concealing its decadence, with a hint of citrus that highlights the floral and nutty poppy seeds. It's a rich, sticky dough, and if you opt to shape it by hand, you'll need extra flour as you handle it. Poppy seeds are notorious for turning rancid on a dime, so give them a whiff—bad ones will smell like bad oil.

Makes 1 loaf

Ingredient	Grams	Volume
Whole milk	120g	1/2 cup
Buttermilk, plain yogurt, or sour cream	120g	1/2 cup
Eggs	100g	2 large
Sugar	55g	1/4 cup
Freshly grated lemon or orange zest	4g	1 tablespoon
Poppy seeds, plus 1 teaspoon (optional) for sprinkling	20g	2 tablespoons
Fine sea salt	10g	1 1/2 teaspoons
Bread flour	455g	3 1/2 cups, spooned and leveled
Unsalted butter, cut into cubes, at room temperature	56g	4 tablespoons
Instant yeast	—	2 teaspoons
Egg white or other crust-browning wash (optional; see page 26)	—	—

Hands-Off Method

In the order listed, add all the ingredients (except for the egg white) to the bread machine's baking pan. Program the machine to its **WHITE** setting and **MEDIUM** crust. Lock the pan into the machine, close the lid, and press **START**. If desired, after the loaf's final rise (usually about 1:30 from completion), brush the loaf with egg white and sprinkle with 1 teaspoon

continued →

Soft Poppy Seed Loaf
continued

poppy seeds. Once complete, remove the bread from the machine. Allow to cool in the pan for 10 to 15 minutes. Then tip the loaf out of the pan onto a cooling rack to cool completely before slicing.

Hand-Shaped Method

In the order listed, add all the ingredients (except for the egg white) to the bread machine's baking pan. Select **DOUGH**, lock the pan into the machine, close the lid, and press **START**. At the completion of the cycle, the dough should be doubled in size; if not, leave it in the machine for additional time as needed.

Transfer the dough to a clean work surface. If it's too sticky to handle, dust it lightly with flour, but resist adding any more than necessary, and use a bench scraper to help lift and move it around. Gently stretch it to a thickness of about 1 inch, then shape it to fit a 9 × 5-inch loaf pan (see page 30, for tips) if baking in a home oven.

Place the loaf seam-side down back in the bread machine pan (or in a greased loaf pan if baking in a home oven). Close the bread machine lid and proof in the bread machine (or cover the loaf pan with a clean towel or food wrap and proof in a warm spot in the kitchen) until doubled in size, about 1 hour. You can also proof the dough overnight in the refrigerator; allow it to warm up at room temperature for 30 to 60 minutes before baking.

To bake in a bread machine: If desired, brush the top of the loaf with egg white and sprinkle with 1 teaspoon poppy seeds. Lock the pan into the bread machine. Select the **BAKE** setting and bake the loaf for 1 hour. Remove the pan from the machine and allow the bread to cool in the pan for 15 minutes. Then tip out onto a cooling rack to cool completely before slicing.

To bake in a home oven: Preheat the oven to 350°F. If desired, brush the top of the loaf with egg white, sprinkle with 1 teaspoon poppy seeds, and score the bread by making a long slash down the length of the loaf with a sharp knife. Bake until nicely browned and hollow-sounding when you tap on the loaf, 40 to 50 minutes.

Cool in the pan for at least 15 minutes. Then tip out onto a cooling rack to cool completely before slicing.

Leftovers and Storage: Best on the day it's made. Stored in an airtight bag or container, the sliced loaf can be frozen for up to 1 month.

Choose-Your-Own-Adventure Swirl Bread

My first cooking job involved bagging sticky cinnamon swirl bread, and while it's true that even the most tempting foods lose their appeal when you're forced to handle them every day, I could never resist that bread. I've re-created it here, with its oozy, toffee-like filling, and a rich, tender bread base that can stand up to it. Given that the bread is a blank canvas for various fillings, I've designed this recipe to be customizable. Cinnamon, jam, chocolate, or caramel . . . only you can decide what happens next!

Makes 1 loaf

Ingredient	Grams	Volume
Whole milk	180g	3/4 cup
Egg	50g	1 large
Egg yolk	18g	1 large
Unsalted butter, melted and slightly cooled	56g	4 tablespoons
Sugar	41g	3 tablespoons
Fine sea salt	10g	1 1/2 teaspoons
Bread flour	390g	3 3/4 cups, spooned and leveled
Instant yeast	—	2 teaspoons
Filling of choice (see page 125)	—	—
Egg white or other crust-browning wash (optional; see page 26)	—	—

continued →

Choose-Your-Own-Adventure Swirl Bread
continued

In the order listed, add all the ingredients (except for the filling and egg white) to the bread machine's baking pan. Select **DOUGH**, lock the pan into the machine, close the lid, and press **START**. At the completion of the cycle, the dough should be doubled in size; if not, leave it in the machine for additional time as needed.

Transfer the dough to a clean work surface. If it's too sticky to handle, dust it lightly with flour, but resist adding any more than necessary, and use a bench scraper to help lift and move it around. Roll it into a 14 × 9-inch rectangle. Cover the surface evenly with your filling of choice, leaving about ½ inch of uncovered dough around the outside.

With a short side (the 9-inch side) facing you, roll the dough into a log, trying not to stretch it too much, and gently tucking the edges into the loaf as you roll to help seal the filling inside. Once you have a log, pinch the seams together.

Place the loaf seam-side down back in the bread machine pan (see Note) or in a greased 9 × 5-inch loaf pan if baking in a home oven. Close the bread machine lid and proof in the bread machine (or cover the loaf pan with a clean towel or food wrap and proof in a warm spot in the kitchen) until doubled in size, about 1 hour. You can also proof the dough overnight in the refrigerator; allow it to warm up at room temperature for 30 to 60 minutes before baking.

To bake in a bread machine: If desired, brush the top of the proofed loaf with egg white and lock the pan into the bread machine. Select the **BAKE** setting and bake the loaf for 1 hour. Remove the pan from the machine and allow the bread to cool in the pan for 15 minutes. Then tip out onto a cooling rack to cool for at least 15 minutes more before slicing. (This is one bread you can eat warm.)

To bake in a home oven: Preheat the oven to 350°F, using convection if available. If desired, brush the top of the loaf with egg white and bake until browned and hollow-sounding when you tap on the loaf or an instant-read thermometer reads 190°F, 40 to 50 minutes. Cool in the pan for at least 15 minutes. Then tip out onto a cooling rack to cool for at least 15 minutes more before slicing. (This is one bread you can eat warm.)

Leftovers and Storage: Best on the day it's made, but leftovers toast well, and the unsliced loaf can be wrapped tightly and frozen for up to 1 month.

Note: If your bread machine produces tall, upright loaves, I recommend making this bread in a loaf pan in your home oven, so that the swirled filling is evenly distributed and clearly pronounced.

Filling Options

Classic Cinnamon Swirl: Stir together **55g (1/4 cup) brown sugar, 55g (1/4 cup) granulated sugar, 8g (1 tablespoon) ground cinnamon**, and a **pinch of salt.** Gently press the mixture onto the rolled-out dough to help it adhere slightly.

Jam and Chocolate Swirl: Using a mini-offset spatula or spoon, spread **100g (about 1/3 cup)** of your **favorite jam** over the rolled-out dough. Sprinkle with **100g (about 2/3 cup) dark chocolate chunks or chopped dark chocolate.** (This is great without the chocolate, too.)

Caramel-Pecan Swirl: Make dulce de leche by submerging **1 (14-ounce) can of sweetened condensed milk**, with its paper label removed, in a large pot of water to cover the can by at least 2 inches. Bring it to a simmer and simmer for 2 1/2 hours, adding more water to keep it submerged if needed. Carefully drain and cool completely. Spread the rolled-out dough with **200g** (a heaping 1/2 cup/about half of the can) **dulce de leche** and sprinkle with **50g (1/2 cup) coarsely chopped toasted pecans**.

French Onion Swirl: In a heavy skillet, cook **1 thinly sliced large onion** in **2 tablespoons butter** or **olive oil** and a few pinches of **salt** until soft, caramelized, and sweet, usually 45 to 60 minutes—don't rush it! Taste for salt and cool completely. Spread the onions over the rolled-out dough and sprinkle with **75g (1 cup) shredded Gruyère, Swiss, or sharp cheddar cheese.**

Pizza Swirl: Using a mini-offset spatula or spoon, spread about **1/4 cup tomato paste** in a thin layer over the rolled-out dough. Sprinkle with **2 teaspoons dried oregano, 150g (1 cup) coarsely shredded low-moisture mozzarella**, and if desired, arrange about **1 cup thinly sliced pepperoni** over the cheese as well.

'90s Swirl: Sprinkle the rolled-out dough with **1/2 cup coarsely chopped, oil-packed sun-dried tomatoes, 1 tablespoon minced fresh or 1 teaspoon dried oregano,** and **115g (4 ounces) crumbled goat cheese.**

5

Natural Tang

Homemade hybrid sourdough optimized for the bread machine, using ripe, homemade sourdough starter and a small amount of commercial yeast. These loaves have an even crumb and a delightful tang—and stay fresher longer than their commercial yeast–only counterparts.

Your Very Own Sourdough Starter

Sourdough starter is what's called a "natural leavener," meaning it can do the work of giving bread its rise, as commercial yeast does in other recipes. And it's actually very simple, just a mixture of flour and water that ferments over time through fresh additions of flour, water, and by interacting with the natural yeast and bacteria all around us.

A small amount of this sourdough starter is typically "fed" with equal parts fresh flour and water to "ripen," during which process it swells with carbon dioxide bubbles and transforms into a looser, more liquid and elastic texture that smells gorgeously tangy, balanced, and alive when done right. This ripe starter then goes into a bread recipe, and as it interacts with the fresh flour and other ingredients, those same bubbles that appeared in the healthy, ripe sourdough starter develop in the bread dough, giving the finished loaf of bread its crumb structure and unique taste.

Making a sourdough starter of your own is truly an easy and forgiving process, and while most instructions, including these, involve very precise measurements of flour and water, there is so much flexibility. As long as you keep adding equal amounts of flour and water when you feed it, you can play around with the types of flours, adjust the proportions of old starter to new flour and water, and continually explore how these things interact and add character in the unique environment of your own kitchen.

Many recipes, including these, use what's called a "100% hydration" sourdough starter, meaning that the starter is made from equal parts flour and water. While many kinds of flour can be used, I tend to stick with all-purpose or bread flour for my base, and find that including a little bit of rye or whole wheat flour does wonders to ensure lots of bubbly activity, particularly when you're first making a starter, or if it's been languishing for a few weeks in the fridge.

Getting Started

Get a set of two wide-mouth, straight-sided jars about 16 ounces in volume, such as 0.5-liter Weck or Le Parfait Familia Wiss Terrine jars. Having two jars means you'll always have a clean one to transfer a fresh feeding in (they can get gunky pretty fast), and the straight-sided jars are easier to reach into with a small spatula.

A silicone mini spatula or spoonula, such as the one made by GIR, makes for easy stirring and scraping against the sides of the jar.

Note: If you're able to procure a little bit of sourdough starter from an avid baker friend, a local bakery, or by sourcing online, you can bypass this step of building your own. Instead, use about a tablespoon (20 grams) of the established starter and feed it immediately, with 50 grams flour (I prefer 40 grams all-purpose and 10 grams rye) and 50 grams water.

Day 1: In a tall jar, mix together 50 grams of tepid water, 40 grams of all-purpose or bread flour, and 10 grams of rye or whole wheat flour. Cover loosely with a lid, without sealing it tightly. Set in a warm spot overnight.

Day 2: You won't see much activity, but the texture should be a bit more liquid. Transfer about a tablespoon (20g) of the mixture to a clean jar and discard the rest. Combine it with another 50 grams water, 40 grams of all-purpose flour, and 10 grams of rye or whole wheat flour. Cover again (not airtight) and leave in a warm spot overnight.

Days 3 through 7: Repeat the same process from Day 2, mixing a little of the previous day's sourdough starter in a clean jar with more flour and water, and begin wrapping a rubber band around the jar to mark the level of the sourdough starter right after new flour and water has been added (i.e., its "feeding"), so that you can easily track its volume growth. By the third or fourth feeding, you should start to notice that it is inflating a bit, and its aroma will become a little fruitier. From this point, you can even feed your starter twice a day to help it build strength more quickly. By Day 7, it should consistently bubble up to about three times its original volume and smell pleasantly ripe. (If it doesn't, just keep feeding it.)

Your sourdough starter will now be strong enough to bake with. After its final feeding and ripening, seal it up and leave it in the fridge. If you expect to bake regularly, feed your starter once a day to keep it strong, using about a tablespoon of this mixture to create your leaven in the sourdough recipes in this book. For less frequent baking, try to remember to feed your starter about once a week, scooping out a spoonful into a clean jar, adding water and flour, and letting it ripen in a warm spot, then transferring the whole thing, sealed up, back to the fridge.

During periods of actively feeding your sourdough starter, save the "discard" in a separate container and use it in sourdough discard recipes, such as the Wheat-y Sourdough Discard Pancakes on page 199.

Wheat-y Sourdough Sandwich Loaf

A go-to, all-purpose sourdough loaf for anyone who maintains a sourdough starter, this has a noticeable wheat-y profile, both in flavor and texture, that complements the gentle tanginess. And its sturdy, moist crumb is ideal for sandwiches and toast. As with all sourdough recipes, the tanginess becomes more pronounced if it has more time to ferment, so when I make this, I often do the bulk fermentation in the refrigerator (see page 28) and bake it in a traditional oven.

Makes 1 loaf

Ingredient	Grams	Volume
Leaven		
Sourdough starter	20g	1 tablespoon
Cool water	40g	2½ tablespoons
All-purpose or bread flour	32g	¼ cup, spooned and leveled
Rye flour or whole wheat flour	8g	1 tablespoon
Dough		
Tepid water	300g	1¼ cups
Olive oil or avocado oil	22g	2 tablespoons
Honey	20g	1 tablespoon
Bread flour	325g	2½ cups, spooned and leveled
Whole wheat or white whole wheat flour	186g	1⅓ cups, spooned and leveled
Fine sea salt	10g	1½ teaspoons
Instant yeast	—	½ teaspoon
Egg white or other crust-browning wash (optional; see page 26)	—	—

continued →

Wheat-y Sourdough Sandwich Loaf

continued

Prepare the leaven: Four to ten hours before baking, in a tall glass or bowl, stir together the sourdough starter with the water and flours. Cover loosely and allow to ripen, until it's roughly tripled in size and is aerated with little bubbles, 4 to 10 hours, depending on the temperature of your kitchen. If you're not ready to bake immediately, seal the jar and transfer the leaven to the refrigerator for up to 10 hours. Don't worry if it has risen and collapsed; just proceed with the recipe.

Make the dough: Scrape the leaven into the bread machine's baking pan. In the order listed, add the dough ingredients (except for the egg white) to the pan. Select **DOUGH**, lock the pan into the machine, close the lid, and press **START**. Leave the dough in the machine as long as necessary until it's doubled in size, which is usually an extra 30 to 90 minutes after the cycle is complete. (See page 26, for tips on doing the bulk rise overnight in the refrigerator.)

Transfer the dough to a clean work surface. If it's too sticky to handle, dust it lightly with flour, but resist adding any more than necessary, and use a bench scraper to help lift and move it around. Gently stretch it to a thickness of about 1 inch, then shape it to fit a 9 × 5-inch loaf pan (see page 30, for tips) if baking in a home oven.

Place the loaf seam-side down back in the bread machine pan (or in a greased loaf pan if baking in a home oven). Close the bread machine lid and proof in the bread machine (or cover the loaf pan with a clean towel or food wrap and proof in a warm spot in the kitchen) until doubled in size, about 1 hour. You can also proof the dough overnight in the refrigerator; allow it to warm up at room temperature for 30 to 60 minutes before baking.

To bake in a bread machine: If desired, brush the top of the proofed loaf with egg white, and lock the pan into the bread machine. Select the **BAKE** setting and bake the loaf for 1 hour. Remove the pan from

Hybrid Sourdough

The sourdough loaves in this chapter are leavened with both sourdough starter and a small amount of commercial yeast, a technique known as "hybrid" sourdough. The yeast helps to make rising and proofing times more consistent for the bread machine, and also to produce a more even crumb. But because the strength of sourdough starters can vary quite a bit, the option for a fully preset baking method isn't included in the recipes in this chapter, as it is elsewhere in the book. Use some of your judgment to ensure the dough is properly risen and proofed before shaping and baking.

the machine and allow the bread to cool in the pan for 15 minutes. Then tip out onto a cooling rack to cool completely before slicing.

To bake in a home oven: Preheat the oven to 350°F, using convection if available. If desired, brush the top of the loaf with egg white, and score the bread by making a long slash down the length of the loaf with a sharp knife. Bake until browned and hollow-sounding when you tap on the loaf or an instant-read thermometer reads 190°F, 40 to 50 minutes. Cool in the pan for at least 15 minutes. Then tip out onto a cooling rack to cool completely before slicing.

Leftovers and Storage: This loaf keeps well for up to 3 days, wrapped loosely at room temperature. Sliced and stored in an airtight bag in the freezer, it keeps for 1 month.

Mild Rye Sourdough Loaf

Even people who aren't crazy about rye bread tend to enjoy this loaf, because the divisive flavor isn't quite as pronounced. (And if the issue is more the caraway seeds than the rye, simply leave them out.) It has a pleasantly light sweetness thanks to the molasses, and the malty notes of rye flour are rounded out by the sourdough starter. I like it thickly sliced, and thickly smeared with good, cold, salted butter and jam.

Makes 1 loaf

Ingredient	Grams	Volume
Leaven		
Sourdough starter	20g	1 tablespoon
Cool water	40g	2½ tablespoons
All-purpose or bread flour	32g	¼ cup, spooned and leveled
Rye flour or whole wheat flour	8g	1 tablespoon
Dough		
Tepid water	120g	½ cup
Whole milk or plant-based milk	120g	½ cup
Molasses	42g	2 tablespoons
Brown sugar or coconut sugar	44g	2 tablespoons
Fine sea salt	10g	1½ teaspoons
Bread flour	400g	3 cups, spooned and leveled
Rye flour	105g	¾ cup, spooned and leveled
Caraway seeds (optional)	7g	1 tablespoon
Instant yeast	—	½ teaspoon
Egg white or other crust-browning wash (optional; see page 26)	—	—

continued →

Mild Rye Sourdough Loaf
continued

Prepare the leaven: Four to ten hours before baking, in a tall glass or bowl, stir together the sourdough starter with the water and flours. Cover loosely and allow to ripen, until it's roughly tripled in size and is aerated with little bubbles, 4 to 10 hours, depending on the temperature of your kitchen. If you're not ready to bake immediately, seal the jar and transfer the leaven to the refrigerator for up to 10 hours. Don't worry if it has risen and collapsed; just proceed with the recipe.

Make the dough: Scrape the leaven into the bread machine's baking pan. In the order listed, add the dough ingredients (except for the egg white) to the pan. Select **DOUGH**, lock the pan into the machine, close the lid, and press **START**. Leave the dough in the machine as long as necessary until it's doubled in size, which is usually an extra 30 to 90 minutes after the cycle is complete. (See page 26, for tips on doing the bulk rise overnight in the refrigerator.)

Transfer the dough to a clean work surface. If it's too sticky to handle, dust it lightly with flour, but resist adding any more than necessary, and use a bench scraper to help lift and move it around. Gently stretch it to a thickness of about 1 inch, then shape it to fit a 9 × 5-inch loaf pan (see page 30, for tips) if baking in a home oven.

Place the loaf seam-side down back in the bread machine pan (or in a greased loaf pan if baking in a home oven). Close the bread machine lid and proof in the bread machine (or cover the loaf pan with a clean towel or food wrap and proof in a warm spot in the kitchen) until doubled in size, about 1 hour. You can also proof the dough overnight in the refrigerator; allow it to warm up at room temperature for 30 to 60 minutes before baking.

To bake in a bread machine: If desired, brush the top of the proofed loaf with egg white and lock the pan into the bread machine. Select the **BAKE** setting and bake the loaf for 1 hour. Remove the pan from the machine and allow the bread to cool in the pan for 15 minutes. Then tip out onto a cooling rack to cool completely before slicing.

To bake in a home oven: Preheat the oven to 350°F, using convection if available. If desired, brush the top of the loaf with egg white, and score the bread by making a long slash down the length of the loaf with a sharp knife. Bake until browned and hollow-sounding when you tap on the loaf or an instant-read thermometer reads 190°F, 40 to 50 minutes. Cool in the pan for at least 15 minutes. Then tip out onto a cooling rack to cool completely before slicing.

Leftovers and Storage: Keeps for up to 3 days, wrapped loosely at room temperature. Stored in an airtight bag or container, the sliced loaf can be frozen for up to 1 month.

Sesame Sourdough Loaf

Sesame oil and whole sesame seeds flavor this loaf with their fragrant, nutty essence, and the tangy sourdough bread base gives it something of an artisan vibe. This is an excellent sandwich loaf for your favorite Italian-style fillings (salty cheese, pickled vegetables, cold cuts), but it's also versatile enough to pair with a broad range of dinner menus. Be sure to use an egg wash (or an alternative wash, see page 26) to ensure the sesame seeds stick to the crust.

Makes 1 loaf

Ingredient	Grams	Volume
Leaven		
Sourdough starter	20g	1 tablespoon
Cool water	40g	2½ tablespoons
All-purpose or bread flour	32g	¼ cup, spooned and leveled
Rye flour or whole wheat flour	8g	1 tablespoon
Dough		
Tepid water	285g	1 cup plus 3 tablespoons
Honey	40g	2 tablespoons
Toasted sesame oil	11g	1 tablespoon
Avocado oil	11g	1 tablespoon
Fine sea salt	10g	1½ teaspoons
Bread flour	390g	3 cups, spooned and leveled
Whole wheat or spelt flour	105g	¾ cup, spooned and leveled
Instant yeast	—	½ teaspoon
Egg white or other crust-browning wash (see page 26)	—	—
Hulled sesame seeds	10g	1 tablespoon

continued →

Sesame Sourdough Loaf

continued

Prepare the leaven: Four to ten hours before baking, in a tall glass or bowl, stir together the sourdough starter with the water and flours. Cover loosely and allow to ripen, until it's roughly tripled in size and is aerated with little bubbles, 4 to 10 hours, depending on the temperature of your kitchen. If you're not ready to bake immediately, seal the jar and transfer the leaven to the refrigerator for up to 10 hours. Don't worry if it has risen and collapsed; just proceed with the recipe.

Make the dough: Scrape the leaven into the bread machine's baking pan. In the order listed, add the dough ingredients (except for the egg white and sesame seeds) to the pan. Select **DOUGH**, lock the pan into the machine, close the lid, and press **START**. Leave the dough in the machine as long as necessary until it's doubled in size, which is usually an extra 30 to 90 minutes after the cycle is complete. (See opposite, for tips on doing the bulk rise overnight in the refrigerator.)

Transfer the dough to a clean work surface. If it's too sticky to handle, dust it lightly with flour, but resist adding any more than necessary, and use a bench scraper to help lift and move it around. Gently stretch it to a thickness of about 1 inch, then shape it to fit a 9 × 5-inch loaf pan (see page 30, for tips) if baking in a home oven.

Place the loaf seam-side down back in the bread machine pan (or in a greased loaf pan if baking in a home oven). Close the bread machine lid and proof in the bread machine (or cover the loaf pan with a clean towel or food wrap and proof in a warm spot in the kitchen) until doubled in size, about 1 hour. You can also proof the dough overnight in the refrigerator; allow it to warm up at room temperature for 30 to 60 minutes before baking.

To bake in a bread machine: Brush the top of the proofed loaf with egg white, sprinkle evenly with the sesame seeds, and lock the pan into the bread machine. Select the **BAKE** setting and bake the loaf for 1 hour. Remove the pan from the machine and allow the bread to cool in the pan for 15 minutes. Then tip out onto a cooling rack to cool completely before slicing.

To bake in a home oven: Preheat the oven to 350°F, using convection if available. Brush the top of the loaf with egg white and sprinkle evenly with the sesame seeds. If desired, score the bread by making a long slash down the

Variation

Pumpkin Seed Loaf: Substitute pumpkin seed oil for the sesame oil and sprinkle the proofed bread with whole pumpkin seeds instead of sesame seeds.

length of the loaf with a sharp knife. Bake until browned and hollow-sounding when you tap on the loaf or an instant-read thermometer reads 190°F, 40 to 50 minutes. Cool in the pan for at least 15 minutes. Then tip out onto a cooling rack to cool completely before slicing.

Leftovers and Storage: Keeps for up to 3 days, wrapped loosely at room temperature. Stored in an airtight bag or container, the sliced loaf can be frozen for up to 1 month.

A Slower Rise

The best loaves of sourdough develop their flavor through a long, cool rise. To do this with these recipes, you can do the bulk rise, or first rise of the bread, in the refrigerator. Remove the dough from the bread machine before it begins proofing and place it in an airtight container—a 2-quart container with straight sides works best, because it's easy to track the progress. Because of the amount of sourdough starter and yeast in these recipes, they need only 6 to 8 hours, so if you wish to let the dough rise longer, reduce the instant yeast by 1/4 teaspoon.

Date & Pecan Sourdough Loaf

As someone with a lifelong aversion to raisins, I'm always inclined to substitute chopped dates when they're called for in cookies and breads. I developed this cinnamon-perfumed loaf with a classic raisin-walnut loaf in mind, with the sourdough base lending tanginess and a moist, more structured crumb. The dates practically melt into it, and the pecans add a snappy texture and sharp hickory notes.

Makes 1 loaf

Ingredient	Grams	Volume
Leaven		
Sourdough starter	20g	1 tablespoon
Cool water	40g	2½ tablespoons
All-purpose or bread flour	32g	¼ cup, spooned and leveled
Rye flour or whole wheat flour	8g	1 tablespoon
Dough		
Tepid water	285g	1 cup plus 3 tablespoons
Honey	40g	2 tablespoons
Fine sea salt	10g	1½ teaspoons
Bread flour	390g	3 cups, spooned and leveled
Whole wheat or white whole wheat flour	105g	¾ cup, spooned and leveled
Unsalted butter, cut into cubes, at room temperature	28g	2 tablespoons
Instant yeast	—	½ teaspoon
Egg white or other crust-browning wash (optional; see page 26)	—	—

continued →

Date & Pecan Sourdough Loaf
continued

Mix-Ins		
Toasted pecans, coarsely chopped	75g	3/4 cup
Pitted dates, coarsely chopped	90g	About 6 large
Ground cinnamon	8g	1 tablespoon
All-purpose or bread flour	—	1 teaspoon

Prepare the leaven: Four to ten hours before baking, in a tall glass or bowl, stir together the sourdough starter with the water and flours. Cover loosely and allow to ripen, until it's roughly tripled in size and is aerated with little bubbles, 4 to 10 hours, depending on the temperature of your kitchen. If you're not ready to bake immediately, seal the jar and transfer the leaven to the refrigerator for up to 10 hours. Don't worry if it has risen and collapsed; just proceed with the recipe.

Make the dough: Scrape the leaven into the bread machine's baking pan. In the order listed, add the dough ingredients (except for the egg white) to the pan. Select **DOUGH**, lock the pan into the machine, close the lid, and press **START**. Leave the dough in the machine as long as necessary until it's doubled in size, which is usually an extra 30 to 90 minutes after the cycle is complete. (See page 26 for tips on doing the bulk rise overnight in the refrigerator.)

Meanwhile, prepare the mix-ins: In a small bowl, combine the pecans, dates, cinnamon, and flour, breaking up any clumps of dates with your fingers.

Transfer the dough to a clean work surface. If it's too sticky to handle, dust it lightly with flour, but resist adding any more than necessary, and use a bench scraper to help lift and move it around. Gently stretch the dough to a thickness of about 3/4 inch and sprinkle with half the pecan/date mixture. Roll it up, then flatten out again and sprinkle with the remaining pecan/date mixture. Gently shape it to fit a 9 × 5-inch loaf pan (see page 30, for tips) if baking in a home oven.

Place the loaf seam-side down back in the bread machine pan (or in a greased loaf pan if

Tip

If your pitted dates are hard and stiff, rather than soft and pliant, soak them in hot water for about 10 minutes. Drain well, then chop them.

baking in a home oven). Close the bread machine lid and proof in the bread machine (or cover the loaf pan with a clean towel or food wrap and proof in a warm spot in the kitchen) until doubled in size, about 1 hour. You can also proof the dough overnight in the refrigerator; allow it to warm up at room temperature for 30 to 60 minutes before baking.

To bake in a bread machine: If desired, brush the top of the proofed loaf with egg white, and lock the pan into the bread machine. Select the **BAKE** setting and bake the loaf for 1 hour. Remove the pan from the machine and allow the bread to cool in the pan for 15 minutes. Then tip out onto a cooling rack to cool completely before slicing.

To bake in a home oven: Preheat the oven to 350°F, using convection if available. If desired, brush the top of the loaf with egg white, and score the bread by making a long slash down the length of the loaf with a sharp knife. Bake until browned and hollow-sounding when you tap on the loaf or an instant-read thermometer reads 190°F, 40 to 50 minutes. Cool in the pan for at least 15 minutes. Then tip out onto a cooling rack to cool completely before slicing.

Leftovers and Storage: Keeps for up to 3 days, wrapped loosely at room temperature. Stored in an airtight bag or container, the sliced loaf can be frozen for up to 1 month.

Variation

Classic Cinnamon-Raisin Sourdough: Substitute 100g (2/3 cup) raisins for the dates, and substitute walnuts for the pecans.

Farro & Spelt Sourdough

Mixing cooked grains into bread dough adds lots of contrast and character—and it's pretty incredible how much cooked grain can be crammed in there. Farro is one of my favorites to use in this way because of its terrific chew, and I love how its toasty flavor amplifies that of the wheat flour. But any nubby cooked grain or rice can be used—I've included some suggestions on page 148.

Makes 1 loaf

Ingredient	Grams	Volume
Leaven		
Sourdough starter	20g	1 tablespoon
Cool water	40g	2½ tablespoons
All-purpose or bread flour	32g	¼ cup, spooned and leveled
Rye flour or whole wheat flour	8g	1 tablespoon
Dough		
Tepid water	285g	1 cup plus 3 tablespoons
Brown sugar	26g	2 tablespoons
Extra-virgin olive oil or avocado oil	22g	2 tablespoons
Fine sea salt	10g	1½ teaspoons
Bread flour	358g	2¾ cups, spooned and leveled
Spelt or whole wheat flour	140g	1 cup, spooned and leveled
Instant yeast	—	½ teaspoon
Cooked farro (recipe follows), cooled	250g	1½ cups
Egg white or other crust-browning wash (optional; see page 26)	—	—

continued →

Farro & Spelt Sourdough
continued

Prepare the leaven: Four to ten hours before baking, in a tall glass or bowl, stir together the sourdough starter with the water and flours. Cover loosely and allow to ripen, until it's roughly tripled in size and is aerated with little bubbles, 4 to 10 hours, depending on the temperature of your kitchen. If you're not ready to bake immediately, seal the jar and transfer the leaven to the refrigerator for up to 10 hours. Don't worry if it has risen and collapsed; just proceed with the recipe.

Make the dough: Scrape the leaven into the bread machine's baking pan. In the order listed, add the dough ingredients (except for the cooked farro and egg white) to the pan. Select **DOUGH**, lock the pan into the machine, close the lid, and press **START**. Leave the dough in the machine as long as necessary until it's doubled in size, which is usually an extra 30 to 90 minutes after the cycle is complete. (See page 26 for tips on doing the bulk rise overnight in the refrigerator.)

Transfer the dough to a clean work surface. If it's too sticky to handle, dust it lightly with flour, but resist adding any more than necessary, and use a bench scraper to help lift and move it around. Stretch the dough to a thickness of about 1 inch, scatter about one-third of the farro over the dough, then roll it up. Repeat this process twice more, until all of the farro is incorporated. (Alternatively, add the farro when the alert for additions sounds during the kneading stage.) Gently shape it to fit a 9 × 5-inch loaf pan (see page 30, for tips) if baking in a home oven.

Place the loaf seam-side down back in the bread machine pan (or in a greased loaf pan if baking in a home oven). Close the bread machine lid and proof in the bread machine (or cover the loaf pan with a clean towel or food wrap and proof in a warm spot in the kitchen) until doubled in size, about 1 hour. You can also proof the dough overnight in the refrigerator; allow it to warm up at room temperature for 30 to 60 minutes before baking.

To bake in a bread machine: If desired, brush the top of the proofed loaf with egg white and lock the pan into the bread machine. Select the **BAKE** setting and bake the loaf for 1 hour. Remove the pan from the machine and allow the bread to cool in the pan for 15 minutes. Then tip out onto a cooling rack to cool completely before slicing.

To bake in a home oven: Preheat the oven to 350°F, using convection if available. If desired, brush the top of the

Variation

To vary the grains, substitute leftover cooked wild rice, brown rice, quinoa, or barley for the farro, by weight (not volume).

loaf with egg white, and score the bread by making a long slash down the length of the loaf with a sharp knife. Bake until browned and hollow-sounding when you tap on the loaf or an instant-read thermometer reads 190°F, 40 to 50 minutes. Cool in the pan for at least 15 minutes. Then tip out onto a cooling rack to cool completely before slicing.

Leftovers and Storage: Keeps for up to 3 days, wrapped loosely. Stored in an airtight bag or container, the sliced loaf can be frozen for up to 1 month.

How to Cook Farro

In a medium saucepan, combine **1 cup rinsed farro** and **3 cups water**. Bring to a boil and add **1/4 teaspoon fine sea salt**. Reduce to a simmer, partially cover, and cook until the grains are tender, about 30 minutes (less if using pearled, or quick-cooking farro). Add a bit more water to the pan if it dries up before the farro is cooked. Drain if necessary. (Alternatively, cook farro in a rice cooker, using the proportions and settings for brown rice.) *Makes about 2 cups (400g).*

Orange Barley Sourdough Loaf with Walnuts

Marmalade infuses orange flavor into this loaf, but it also captures the singular bitterness of the fruit's rind, with little bits woven into the crumb. It's a lovely profile with a sourdough base, and a perfect foil to the soft, sweet barley flour.

Makes 1 loaf

Ingredient	Grams	Volume
Leaven		
Sourdough starter	20g	1 tablespoon
Cool water	40g	2½ tablespoons
All-purpose or bread flour	32g	¼ cup, spooned and leveled
Rye flour or whole wheat flour	8g	1 tablespoon
Dough		
Tepid water	240g	1 cup
Finely grated orange zest (from 1 orange)	—	About 1 tablespoon
Orange marmalade	100g	¼ cup
Fine sea salt	10g	1½ teaspoons
Bread flour	357g	2¾ cups, spooned and leveled
Barley flour	120g	1 cup, spooned and leveled
Unsalted butter or vegan butter, cut into cubes, at room temperature	42g	3 tablespoons
Instant yeast	—	½ teaspoon
Coarsely chopped toasted walnuts	90g	¾ cup
Egg white or other crust-browning wash (optional; see page 26)	—	—

continued →

Orange Barley Sourdough Loaf with Walnuts

continued

Prepare the leaven: Four to ten hours before baking, in a tall glass or bowl, stir together the sourdough starter with the water and flours. Cover loosely and allow to ripen, until it's roughly tripled in size and is aerated with little bubbles, 4 to 10 hours, depending on the temperature of your kitchen. If you're not ready to bake immediately, seal the jar and transfer the leaven to the refrigerator for up to 10 hours. Don't worry if it has risen and collapsed; just proceed with the recipe.

Make the dough: Scrape the leaven into the bread machine's baking pan. In the order listed, add the dough ingredients (except for the walnuts and egg white) to the pan. Select **DOUGH**, lock the pan into the machine, close the lid, and press **START**. Leave the dough in the machine as long as necessary until it's doubled in size, which is usually an extra 30 to 90 minutes after the cycle is complete. (See page 26 for tips on doing the bulk rise overnight in the refrigerator.)

Transfer the dough to a clean work surface. If it's too sticky to handle, dust it lightly with flour, but resist adding any more than necessary, and use a bench scraper to help lift and move it around. Stretch the dough to a thickness of about 1 inch, scatter about half of the walnuts over the dough, then roll it up. Repeat this process once more, until all of the walnuts are incorporated. (Alternatively, add them when the alert for additions sounds during the kneading stage.) Gently shape it to fit a 9 × 5-inch loaf pan (see page 30, for tips) if baking in a home oven.

Place the loaf seam-side down back in the bread machine pan (or in a greased loaf pan if baking in a home oven). Close the bread machine lid and proof in the bread machine (or cover the loaf pan with a clean towel or food wrap and proof in a warm spot in the kitchen) until doubled in size, about 1 hour. You can also proof the dough overnight in the refrigerator; allow it to warm up at room temperature for 30 to 60 minutes before baking.

To bake in a bread machine: If desired, brush the top of the proofed loaf with egg white and lock the pan into the bread machine. Select the **BAKE** setting and bake the loaf for 1 hour. Remove the pan from the machine and allow the bread to cool in the pan for 15 minutes. Then tip out onto a cooling rack to cool completely before slicing.

To bake in a home oven: Preheat the oven to 350°F, using convection if available. If desired, brush the top of the loaf with egg white, and score the bread by making a long slash down the length of the loaf with a sharp knife. Bake until browned and hollow-sounding when you tap on the loaf or an instant-read thermometer reads 190°F, 40 to 50 minutes. Cool in the pan for at least 15 minutes. Then tip out onto a cooling rack to cool completely before slicing.

Leftovers and Storage: Keeps for up to 3 days, wrapped loosely at room temperature. Stored in an airtight bag or container, the sliced loaf can be frozen for up to 1 month.

Variation

Orange Barley Sourdough Dinner Rolls: After incorporating the walnuts, divide the dough into 15 portions and follow the shaping, proofing, and baking instructions for Ranch Rolls (page 163).

6

Loaf Adjacent

Keeper recipes that capitalize on the bread machine's handy hands-free Dough program—for low-stress pizza nights, holiday cinnamon rolls made while multitasking, and buttermilk dinner rolls that steal the spotlight from Thanksgiving turkey.

Whole Wheat Sheet Pan Pizza Dough

Once I began to appreciate the flavor that whole wheat flour adds to pizza dough, I've found it hard to go back to a crust made only from white flour. This is a dough you can make ahead of time if you wish—portions can be refrigerated for up to a few days, or frozen for a month. It takes well to any of your favorite toppings, and I've included some of my own as well.

Makes enough for 2 sheet pan pizzas

Ingredient	Grams	Volume
Cool water	480g	2 cups
Bread flour	390g	3 cups, spooned and leveled
Whole wheat or white whole wheat flour	210g	1½ cups, spooned and leveled
Fine sea salt	15g	2¼ teaspoons
Instant yeast	—	½ teaspoon
Extra-virgin olive oil, for greasing	—	—

In the order listed, add all the ingredients (except for the olive oil) to the bread machine's baking pan. Select **DOUGH**, lock the pan into the machine, close the lid, and press **START**. Leave the dough in the machine as long as necessary until it's doubled in size, which is usually an extra 1 to 3 hours after the cycle is complete.

Transfer the dough to a clean work surface. If it's too sticky to handle, dust the dough and your work surface lightly with flour, but resist adding any more than necessary, using a bench scraper to help get underneath the dough, and divide into 2 equal portions. Shape each one into a ball by cupping your hands over the dough and rubbing its base against the work surface in a circle, using the friction it generates to seal up the seam and make the ball smooth and taut.

If cooking the pizzas immediately, cover the shaped dough with a clean towel and allow to proof until slightly puffed, 20 to 30 minutes. Otherwise put the shaped dough in airtight containers with room to expand to more than double in size and refrigerate for up to 3 days or freeze for a month, until ready to use. Thaw overnight in the refrigerator if working with frozen dough.

continued →

Whole Wheat Sheet Pan Pizza Dough

continued

Preheat the oven to 450°F, letting it fully heat up for at least 45 minutes. If you have a baking stone or steel, place it on the top rack of your oven to preheat as well.

Generously grease two 18 × 13-inch sheet pans with olive oil, enough to liberally coat, and place the dough in the center. Use your hands to gently stretch the dough, flipping it in the oil as necessary, to cover as much of the surface as possible (it'll puff and spread further in the oven). If it keeps recoiling, allow it to rest for 5 to 10 minutes to relax.

Arrange your toppings on the dough (see Pizza Toppings, opposite, for some ideas), then slide into the hot oven and bake until the pizza is blistered, bronzed, and cooked evenly on the base, 20 to 25 minutes. If using a pizza stone or steel, it's best to bake the pizzas one at a time.

Leftovers: Wrap leftovers in foil and reheat in a 350°F oven, until warmed all the way through.

Variation

Sourdough Pizza Crust: Prepare a leaven by combining 20g sourdough starter, 40g cool water, 32g all-purpose flour, and 8g rye or whole wheat flour in a tall glass or bowl; leave to ripen in a warm spot until tripled in size. Add to the bread machine along with the pizza dough ingredients, omitting the yeast, and proceed with the recipe. Allow extra time for the first rise until the dough is doubled in size.

Pizza Toppings

Potato-Rosemary Pizza

Thinly slice **1 pound Yukon Gold potatoes** (no need to peel) and soak in plenty of warm, salted water for 30 to 60 minutes. Drain and blot dry, then toss with **3 tablespoons avocado oil** and spread over the prepared dough. Sprinkle with **a few pinches of salt, leaves from 2 sprigs rosemary,** and **freshly ground black pepper.** Bake, then drizzle with **extra-virgin olive oil** just before serving.

Spicy Honey Pizza

Dab about **¼ cup tomato paste** and up **to 2 tablespoons harissa** over the crust, then use a spoon or small offset spatula to combine and spread evenly all over. Scatter with **2 balls torn burrata** or **2 cups shredded low-moisture mozzarella** and drizzle with **1 to 2 tablespoons honey** or **hot honey.** Sprinkle with salt and bake.

Tomato Mozzarella Pizza

Make a simple pizza sauce by combining **1 (28-ounce) can crushed tomatoes, 3 tablespoons olive oil, ½ teaspoon fine sea salt, 2 teaspoons dried oregano,** and **a pinch of sugar** in a medium saucepan. Bring to a gentle simmer and cook until slightly thickened, 20 to 30 minutes. Cool. Cover your pizza with about **2 cups shredded low-moisture mozzarella,** then spoon the sauce on top of the cheese (this prevents the crust from getting soggy). Sprinkle **grated Parmesan cheese** on top and bake.

Pesto, Zucchini, and Burrata Pizza

Spread the dough with **6 to 8 tablespoons pesto, 2 balls torn burrata,** and **1 medium zucchini**, sliced about ¼ inch thick. Sprinkle with **salt,** drizzle lightly with **olive oil,** and bake.

Semolina Focaccia

Focaccia is an inherently unfussy bread, and even if you have a favorite easy method, you'll find the bread machine streamlines the simple process even further. I'm partial to recipes that use semolina flour in the dough—it's traditionally a flour for pasta making because of its high protein content, but here it adds extra chew to the bread without compromising on its loftiness. It even adds a bit of creaminess to the flavor and mouthfeel.

Makes 1 focaccia

Ingredient	Grams	Volume
Dough		
Tepid water	360g	1½ cups
Fine sea salt	10g	1½ teaspoons
Honey	5g	1 teaspoon
Bread flour	358g	2¾ cups
Semolina flour	105g	¾ cup
Instant yeast	—	1½ teaspoons
Assembly		
Butter or cooking spray, for greasing	—	—
Extra-virgin olive oil	55g	5 tablespoons
Water	—	1 tablespoon
Flaky salt, for sprinkling	—	—

Make the dough: In the order listed, add all the ingredients to the bread machine's baking pan. Select DOUGH. Lock the pan into the machine, close the lid, and press START. At the completion of the cycle, the dough should be doubled in size; if not, leave it in the machine for additional time as needed.

To assemble: Grease a metal 9 × 13-inch cake pan or quarter-sheet pan with butter or cooking spray. Gently scrape the dough onto the baking

continued →

Semolina Focaccia
continued

sheet and drizzle with 3 tablespoons of the olive oil. Stretch it out to cover about 60 percent of the surface of the pan. Cover the pan loosely with reusable food wrap or plastic wrap and leave in a warm place to double again in size, about 1 hour.

Preheat the oven to 425°F, using convection if available.

In a small bowl or cup, whisk together the remaining 2 tablespoons olive oil and the water until emulsified.

Moisten your fingers and press them into the dough, poking it all over and aiming to flatten and stretch it into an even thickness that covers as much of the pan as you can. Drizzle the oil/water mixture over the bread, letting it trickle into the dimples. Sprinkle with flaky salt.

Transfer to the oven and bake until golden brown on top and evenly browned on the bottom (tuck a spatula underneath to check the progress), 20 to 30 minutes. Cool for at least 15 minutes before cutting into the bread.

Leftovers and Storage:
Best on the day it's made. Leftovers can be frozen for up to 1 month. To reheat, wrap in foil and warm in a 350°F oven for 10 to 15 minutes.

Ranch Rolls

Meet your newest Thanksgiving menu nonnegotiable. These are fluffy and rich, and unfurl in buttery strands as you tear in. But what's most distinctive is the medley of herbs in the dough and the tangy sprinkle of seasoning mix on top, which play on the flavor of classic ranch salad dressing. The bread machine makes them incredibly effortless to throw together, and while they must be shaped by hand, the soft dough is easy to handle.

Makes 15 dinner rolls

Ingredient	Grams	Volume
Dough		
Cool water	160g	2/3 cup
Buttermilk	160g	2/3 cup
Sugar	42g	3 tablespoons
Fine sea salt	10g	1 1/2 teaspoons
Bread flour	433g	3 1/3 cups
Dried parsley	—	1 tablespoon
Garlic powder	—	1 teaspoon
Dill weed or dill seed	—	1/2 teaspoon
Unsalted butter or vegan butter, cut into 1/2-inch cubes, at room temperature	28g	2 tablespoons
Instant yeast	—	2 teaspoons
Egg white or other crust-browning wash (see page 26)	—	—
Topping		
Unsalted butter, melted	28g	2 tablespoons
Dry ranch dressing mix (1 packet)	28g	2 tablespoons

continued →

Ranch Rolls
continued

Make the dough: In the order listed, add all the ingredients (except for the egg white) to the bread machine's baking pan. Select **DOUGH**, lock the pan into the machine, close the lid, and press **START**. At the completion of the cycle, the dough should be doubled in size; if not, leave it in the machine for additional time as needed.

Shape the rolls: Transfer the dough to a clean work surface. It shouldn't require any extra flour for handling; use a bench scraper to help lift and move it around. Divide the dough into 15 equal portions (see Note). Working one at a time, shape into a ball and then cup your hand over the round and rub it in a circle against the work surface, using the friction it generates to seal up the seam and make the roll smooth and taut.

Arrange the shaped rolls on a well-buttered 9 × 13-inch metal baking pan or quarter-sheet pan, in a grid of 5 rolls by 3. Cover loosely with a clean kitchen towel. Proof the rolls until doubled in size, about 1 hour at room temperature, or 4 to 8 hours in the refrigerator. If refrigerating, allow the rolls to warm up for 30 to 60 minutes before baking.

Preheat the oven to 400°F.

Brush the proofed rolls gently with egg white. Transfer to the oven and bake until golden brown on their tops and their bases (tuck a spatula underneath one to check), 20 to 25 minutes.

Top the rolls: Right out of the oven, brush the rolls with melted butter, then use a small sieve to sprinkle the ranch dressing mix on top. (Alternatively, brush the rolls with butter, then transfer to a serving platter; sprinkle with the dressing mix and gently toss the rolls to coat all over.)

Serve warm or at room temperature.

Leftovers and Storage: These are best on the day they're made, but can be frozen for up to 1 month. To rewarm them, wrap the rolls in foil and place in a 300°F oven for 10 to 15 minutes.

Note: For uniformly sized portions of dough, weigh the proofed dough on a digital scale and divide it by the number of portions you'll need (e.g., 1,000 grams of dough divided by 10 rolls = 100 grams per roll). Then start by eyeballing the portions as you cut the dough, but weigh each out before shaping.

Variation

Classic Buttermilk Rolls: Omit the herbs and dressing mix. After brushing the proofed rolls with egg wash, sprinkle with your choice of garnishes, such as sesame seeds, poppy seeds, flaky salt, or everything bagel seasoning. The baked rolls don't need to be brushed with melted butter.

Summer Hoagies

My summers growing up were marked by swim meets and camping outings, and a fixture of lunches during those activities were sandwiches made on store-bought hoagie rolls—wrapped tightly in plastic wrap so that the distinct components melded into one unit. These are an homage to those. Because a hoagie is a bread-forward sandwich, fill with punchy pickled peppers and other strongly flavored condiments. This recipe works great for classic hamburger buns, too (see the Variation on page 168).

Makes 8 hoagie rolls

Ingredient	Grams	Volume
Cool water	240g	1 cup
Whole milk or plant-based milk, plus more for brushing	80g	1/3 cup
Sugar	28g	2 tablespoons
Fine sea salt	10g	1 1/2 teaspoons
Bread flour	480g	3 1/3 cups
Unsalted butter or vegan butter, cut into cubes, at room temperature	28g	2 tablespoons
Instant yeast	—	2 teaspoons
Egg white or other crust-browning wash (see page 26)	—	—
Toasted sesame seeds, everything bagel seasoning, poppy seeds, or shichimi togarashi, for topping	—	About 2 tablespoons

continued →

Summer Hoagies
continued

In the order listed, add all the ingredients (except for the egg white and toppings) to the bread machine's baking pan. Select **DOUGH**, lock the pan into the machine, close the lid, and press **START**. At the completion of the cycle, the dough should be doubled in size; if not, leave it in the machine for additional time as needed.

If it's too sticky to handle, dust the dough lightly with flour, but resist adding any more than necessary, which will make the rolls hard to shape, and use a bench scraper to help lift and move it around. Divide the dough into 8 equal portions. Working with one at a time, flatten a piece into a rough rectangle, then roll it into a small, tight log 4 to 5 inches long. Rub its base back and forth against the work surface, using the friction it generates to seal up the seam and make the roll smooth and taut.

Arrange the shaped rolls on a parchment-lined baking sheet, spacing them out by about 3 inches. Cover loosely with a clean kitchen towel. Proof the rolls until doubled in size, about 1 hour at room temperature, or 4 to 8 hours in the refrigerator. If refrigerating, allow the rolls to warm up for 20 to 30 minutes before baking.

Preheat the oven to 375°F.

Brush the proofed rolls gently with egg white and sprinkle with your toppings of choice. Transfer to the oven and bake until golden brown on their tops and their bases (tuck a spatula underneath one to check), 25 to 30 minutes.

Allow to cool completely before slicing in half, using a serrated knife.

Leftovers and Storage: Rolls keep well for 2 days, wrapped loosely at room temperature. Stored in an airtight bag or container, the individual rolls can be frozen for up to 1 month.

Variation

Hamburger Buns: Divide the dough into 8 or 10 equal portions (8 for large buns, 10 for smaller ones). Working one portion at a time, cup your hand over the dough and rub in a circle against the work surface, using the friction to seal up their seams and make them smooth and taut balls. Arrange on a parchment-lined baking sheet, spacing them out by about 2 inches. Proceed with proofing and baking as directed.

Brown Sugar & Tahini Swirl Buns

Including a bit of whole wheat flour and enriching the filling and glaze with nutty, buttery tahini, somehow just adds to the built-in decadence of my adaptation of a cinnamon roll. This is an easy-to-work-with dough that may at first seem a little too stiff, but it rolls out and cuts beautifully, with satisfying, distinct spirals, and then bakes to pillowy perfection. The shaped rolls freeze really well for preparing in advance (see Note).

Makes 12 buns

Ingredient	Grams	Volume
Dough		
Whole milk	180g	3/4 cup
Unsalted butter, melted, plus more for the baking pan	56g	4 tablespoons
Eggs	100g	2 large
Granulated sugar	55g	1/4 cup
Fine sea salt	8g	1 1/4 teaspoons
Bread flour	390g	3 cups, spooned and leveled
Whole wheat or white whole wheat flour	105g	3/4 cup, spooned and leveled
Instant yeast	—	2 teaspoons
Filling		
Unsalted butter, melted	56g	4 tablespoons
Tahini, well stirred	45g	3 tablespoons
Brown sugar	165g	3/4 cup
Ground cinnamon	—	2 teaspoons
Fine sea salt	—	Pinch

continued →

Brown Sugar & Tahini Swirl Buns
continued

Glaze		
Powdered sugar, sifted	60g	½ cup
Tahini, well stirred	15g	1 tablespoon
Maple syrup	20g	1 tablespoon
Whole milk	15g to 30g	1 to 2 tablespoons
Fine sea salt	—	Pinch

Make the dough: In the order listed, add all the dough ingredients to the bread machine's baking pan. Select DOUGH, lock the pan into the machine, close the lid, and press START. At the completion of the cycle, the dough should be doubled in size; if not, leave it in the machine for additional time as needed.

Make the filling: In a small bowl, stir together the melted butter, tahini, brown sugar, cinnamon, and salt until smooth.

Liberally grease a metal 9 × 13-inch baking pan or quarter-sheet pan with butter.

Transfer the dough to a clean work surface. It shouldn't require any extra flour for handling; use a bench scraper to help lift and move it around. Roll it into a rectangle about 10 × 15 inches. With a long side facing you, spread the filling evenly over the dough, using a mini-offset spatula or the back of the spoon. Starting at a long side, roll it into a tight log. Use a sharp knife to cut the log crosswise into 12 rolls.

Arrange the rolls on the prepared pan, in a grid of 3 by 4 rolls. Cover lightly with food wrap and allow to proof until puffed up and roughly doubled in size, about 1 hour at room temperature, or 6 to 8 hours in the refrigerator.

Preheat the oven to 350°F, using convection if available.

Bake the proofed rolls until lightly browned at the edges and the filling is bubbling in spots, 25 to 30 minutes. Cool for at least 10 minutes.

Meanwhile, make the glaze: In a small bowl, whisk together the powdered sugar, tahini, maple syrup, 1 tablespoon of the milk, and salt until smooth. It should be an easy-to-drizzle consistency; add additional milk or powdered sugar as needed to thin or thicken it.

Drizzle the glaze over the warm rolls and serve them hot, warm, or at room temperature.

Storage and Leftovers: Best on the day they are made. Leftovers can be wrapped in foil and reheated for 10 to 15 minutes in a 350°F oven. The shaped rolls can be frozen for up to 1 month, then thawed overnight in the refrigerator, proofed, and baked.

Bread Machine Bagels

A bread machine does very well at kneading bagel dough, and as a longtime New York City resident with an abundance of excellent bagel options within walking distance of my apartment, I've been surprised and delighted to discover how delicious and satisfying they are to make from scratch. At home, you're more likely to achieve the elusive, optimal balance of crispy crust and chewy inside. This is project baking, but it's not as complicated as you might think.

Makes 8 bagels

Ingredient	Grams	Volume
Dough		
Cool water	350g	Scant 1½ cups
Barley malt syrup (see Note) or brown sugar	14g	1 tablespoon
Fine sea salt	10g	1½ teaspoons
Bread flour	590g	4½ cups, spooned and leveled
Instant yeast	—	2 teaspoons
To Finish		
Barley malt syrup or brown sugar	—	¼ cup
Baking soda	—	1 teaspoon
Sesame seeds, poppy seeds, or everything bagel seasoning	—	About ¼ cup

continued →

Bread Machine Bagels

continued

Make the dough: In the order listed, add the dough ingredients to the bread machine's baking pan. Select **DOUGH**, lock the pan into the machine, close the lid, and press **START**. At the completion of the cycle, the dough should be doubled in size; if not, leave it in the machine for additional time as needed.

Transfer the dough to a clean work surface. It shouldn't require any extra flour for handling; use a bench scraper to help lift and move it around. Divide into 8 equal portions and roll each one into a ball by cupping your hand over the dough and rubbing its base against the work surface in a circle, using the friction to seal up the seam and make the ball smooth and taut. Cover loosely with a clean towel and let the shaped balls rest for 5 to 10 minutes.

Meanwhile, line two baking sheets with parchment paper.

Working one by one, poke a hole in the center of each ball, and then use your two index fingers to stretch them into bagel shapes, spinning them like bicycle pedals until they're a little less than 1 inch in thickness. Arrange the bagels on the parchment-lined baking sheets. Cover with plastic wrap and allow to proof until doubled in size, about 1 hour at room temperature or overnight in the refrigerator. If proofing overnight in the refrigerator, allow them to warm up at room temperature for about 30 to 60 minutes before proceeding.

Preheat the oven to 450°F, positioning two racks in the oven, one in the lower third and the other in the upper third.

Fill your largest pot halfway with water and bring to a boil. Stir in the barley malt syrup (or brown sugar) and baking soda.

Variations

Sourdough Bagels: Prepare a leaven by combining 20g sourdough starter, 40g cool water, 32g all-purpose flour, and 8g rye or whole wheat flour in a tall glass or bowl; leave to ripen in a warm spot until tripled in size. Add to the bread machine pan along with the following modifications: Reduce the water to 300g (1¼ cups), bread flour to 550g (4 cups plus 2 tablespoons), and instant yeast to ¼ teaspoon. Allow extra time for the first rise and for proofing the dough and shaped bagels until doubled in size.

Whole Wheat Bagels: Substitute 140g (1 cup) whole wheat or white whole wheat flour for 140g (1 cup plus 2 teaspoons) of the bread flour.

If adding toppings to your bagels, spread 3 to 4 tablespoons of each one on shallow bowls or plates.

Adding as many bagels as will fit comfortably in a single layer (usually 2 or 3), lower the bagels into the boiling water and cook for 1 minute. Flip them and boil for 1 minute more. Use a slotted spoon or spider skimmer to lift from the water to drain, then dredge in your toppings, if using. Return the parcooked and topped bagels to the parchment-lined sheets.

Bake the bagels until well browned and crisp, 25 to 30 minutes, switching the pans between the oven racks and flipping the bagels over halfway through. Allow to cool for at least 20 minutes before slicing in half with a serrated knife and eating.

Leftovers and Storage: Best on the day they're made, though day-old bagels can be revived by toasting. Freeze in an airtight bag or container for up to 1 month.

Note: Barley malt syrup gives bagels their unique flavor, and can be easily sourced online. But brown sugar is a fine substitute in its absence.

7

Light, Yeasted Desserts

Not-too-sweet desserts that straddle the bread-cake divide. Inspired by cakes made before the advent of baking powder, the bread machine's Quick or Rapid setting activates yeast for leavening, making freshly baked dessert as easy as pressing a button.

Yeasted Buckwheat Cake

Reminiscent of coffee cake but much lighter than the streusel-topped version, this cake is flecked with purple-y buckwheat and has a fragrant, buttery aroma. The brown sugar topping caramelizes all over, forming a brittle, crazy-good, sugary crust. To maximize it for each serving, slice it not like bread but like sheet cake, into wedges or rectangles.

Makes 1 cake

Ingredient	Grams	Volume
Topping		
Brown sugar, light or dark	55g	1/4 cup
Unsalted butter, cut into cubes, cold	28g	2 tablespoons
Fine sea salt	—	Big pinch
Cake		
Whole milk, cold	120g	1/2 cup
Eggs	100g	2 large
Vanilla extract	—	2 teaspoons
Granulated sugar	55g	1/4 cup
Fine sea salt	5g	1/2 teaspoon
Bread flour	260g	2 cups, spooned and leveled
Buckwheat flour	35g	1/4 cup, spooned and leveled
Unsalted butter, cut into cubes, at room temperature	56g	4 tablespoons
Instant yeast	—	2 teaspoons

continued →

Yeasted Buckwheat Cake
continued

Make the topping: In a small bowl, combine the brown sugar, butter, and salt and use your fingers to mix them together until moist crumbles form. Store in the refrigerator until it's time to use.

To bake in a bread machine: In the order listed, add the cake ingredients to the bread machine's baking pan. Program the machine to its QUICK or RAPID WHITE setting and MEDIUM crust. Lock the pan into the machine, close the lid, and press START. Near the time that your dough begins its final rise (usually about 1:30 from completion), open your machine and scatter the topping evenly over the top of the loaf. Once the baking cycle is complete, remove the bread from the machine and tip the loaf out of the pan onto a cooling rack and cool for at least 15 minutes before slicing.

To bake in a home oven: In the order listed, add all the cake ingredients to the bread machine's baking pan. Select DOUGH, lock the pan into the machine, close the lid, and press START. At the completion of the cycle, the dough should be doubled in size; if not, leave it in the machine for additional time as needed.

Transfer the dough to a well-buttered 8- or 9-inch cake pan, using greased hands to gently stretch and shape it to fill the pan, without deflating it too much (it will be a wet dough). Cover loosely with food wrap and allow to proof in a warm spot in the kitchen until doubled in size, 45 to 60 minutes.

Meanwhile, preheat the oven to 350°F.

Sprinkle the topping over the proofed dough. Transfer to the oven and bake until domed and set in the center, 35 to 45 minutes. Cool for at least 15 minutes in the pan before slicing and serving.

Leftovers and Storage: Best on the day it's made. Revive leftovers by wrapping in foil and rewarming in a 300°F oven for 10 to 15 minutes. Stored in an airtight bag or container, the sliced cake can be frozen for up to 1 month.

Yeasted Yogurt Cake

Yogurt gives this tangy, fragrant cake's soft crumb a fluffy quality, and to best achieve this texture, you'll want to use regular yogurt, not the thick Greek style. But if that's all you've got, thin it with a bit of milk or water so that it's lighter in consistency. While cakes like this tend to dry out rather quickly and are best on the day they're made, day-old slices make an excellent base for French Toast (see page 198).

Makes 1 loaf cake

Ingredient	Grams	Volume
Cake		
Plain whole-milk or nondairy yogurt (not Greek-style)	240g	1 cup
Eggs	100g	2 large
Almond or vanilla extract		2 teaspoons
Sugar	110g	1/2 cup
Avocado or mild-tasting olive oil	45g	1/4 cup
Grated zest of 1 orange, lime, or lemon	—	—
Fine sea salt	8g	3/4 teaspoon
Bread flour	455g	3 1/2 cups, spooned and leveled
Instant yeast	—	2 teaspoons
Topping		
Sugar	26g	1/4 cup

continued →

Yeasted Yogurt Cake

continued

To bake in a bread machine: In the order listed, add the cake ingredients to the bread machine's baking pan. Program the machine to its **QUICK** or **RAPID WHITE** setting and **MEDIUM** crust. Lock the pan into the machine, close the lid, and press **START**. Near the time that your dough begins its final rise (usually about 1:30 from completion), open your machine and sprinkle the sugar topping evenly over the loaf. Once the baking cycle is complete, remove the bread from the machine and tip the loaf out of the pan onto a cooling rack and cool for at least 15 minutes before slicing.

To bake in a home oven: In the order listed, add the cake ingredients to the bread machine's baking pan. Select **DOUGH**, lock the pan into the machine, close the lid, and press **START**. At the completion of the cycle, the dough should be doubled in size; if not, leave it in the machine for additional time as needed.

Transfer the dough to a well-greased 8- or 9-inch cake pan, using greased hands to gently stretch and shape it to fill the pan, without deflating it too much (it will be a wet dough). Cover loosely with food wrap and allow to proof in a warm spot in the kitchen until doubled in size, 45 to 60 minutes. Meanwhile, preheat the oven to 350°F.

Sprinkle the topping sugar over the proofed dough, then transfer to the oven and bake until domed and set in the center, 35 to 45 minutes.

Cool for at least 15 minutes in the pan before slicing and serving.

Leftovers and Storage: Best on the day it's made. Revive leftovers by wrapping in foil and rewarming in a 300°F oven for 10 to 15 minutes, or use them for French Toast (page 198). Stored in an airtight bag or container, the sliced cake can be frozen for up to 1 month.

Dark Chocolate & Olive Oil Loaf

This earthy chocolate loaf balloons like a brioche while baking, and has a similarly pillowy crumb, but with a fragrant, slightly bitter sweetness and enticing chunks of dark chocolate studded throughout it. Olive oil is a perfect pair, and a good-quality one is noticed here. Leftovers make for extremely festive Bread Pudding (page 197), and while it's a dessert loaf, it counterbalances savory, salty dishes at breakfast, too.

Makes 1 loaf

Ingredient	Grams	Volume
Tepid water	210g	3/4 cup plus 2 tablespoons
Eggs	100g	2 large
Sugar	80g	6 tablespoons
Extra-virgin olive oil	44g	1/4 cup
Fine sea salt	10g	1 1/2 teaspoons
Bread flour	488g	3 3/4 cups, spooned and leveled
Cocoa powder, preferably Dutch-process	23g	1/3 cup
Instant yeast	—	2 teaspoons
Coarsely chopped dark chocolate (70% cacao)	170g	1 cup
Egg white or other crust-browning wash (optional; see page 26)	—	—

continued →

Dark Chocolate & Olive Oil Loaf
continued

To bake in a bread machine: In the order listed, add all the ingredients (except for the dark chocolate and egg white) to the bread machine's baking pan. Program the machine to its **WHITE** setting and **MEDIUM** crust. Lock the pan into the machine, close the lid, and press **START**. When the alert for additions sounds, add the chocolate. If desired, after the loaf's final rise (usually around 1:30 from completion), pause the program and brush the proofed loaf with egg wash. Once complete, remove the bread from the machine to cool for 10 to 15 minutes. Then tip the loaf out of the pan onto a cooling rack. Cool completely before slicing.

To bake in a home oven: In the order listed, add all the ingredients (except for the dark chocolate and egg white) to the bread machine's baking pan. Select **DOUGH**, lock the pan into the machine, close the lid, and press **START**. When the alert for additions sounds, add the chocolate. At the completion of the cycle, the dough should be doubled in size; if not, leave it in the machine for additional time as needed.

Transfer the dough to a clean work surface. If it's too sticky to handle, dust it lightly with flour, but resist adding any more than necessary, and use a bench scraper to help lift and move it around. Gently stretch it to a thickness of about 1 inch, then shape it to fit a 9 × 5-inch loaf pan (see page 30, for tips).

Place it seam-side down in a greased loaf pan. Cover with a clean towel or food wrap and proof in a warm spot in the kitchen until doubled in size, about 1 hour. You can also proof the dough overnight in the refrigerator; allow it to warm up at room temperature for 30 to 60 minutes before baking.

Preheat the oven to 350°F, using convection if available.

If desired, brush the top of the bread with egg white. Bake until browned and hollow-sounding when you tap on the loaf or an instant-read thermometer reads 190°F, 40 to 50 minutes.

Cool in the pan for at least 15 minutes. Then tip out onto a cooling rack to cool completely before slicing.

Leftovers and Storage: Keeps for up to 2 days, wrapped loosely at room temperature. Stored in an airtight bag or container, the sliced loaf can be frozen for up to 1 month.

Variations

Chocolate Cherry Loaf: Reduce the chopped chocolate to 75g (1/2 cup) and add 75g (1/2 cup) dried cherries.

Orange-Scented Chocolate Loaf: Along with the wet ingredients, add 1 teaspoon orange blossom water and the grated zest of 1 orange, and replace 75g (1/2 cup) of the chopped chocolate with 75g (1/2 cup) dried mandarin oranges, coarsely chopped.

Gingery Apple Cake

A little bit chewy, a little bit sweet, and heady with cool-weather spices, this yeasted cake fills the kitchen with fall aromas. Coarsely grated apple is added directly into the batter, adding sweetness, moisture, and a subtle perfume.

Makes 1 loaf cake

Ingredient	Grams	Volume
Topping		
Granulated sugar	55g	1/4 cup
Unsalted butter, cut into 1/2-inch cubes, cold,	28g	2 tablespoons
Fine sea salt	—	Big pinch
Cake		
Coarsely grated peeled apple (1 medium)	140g	1 cup
Whole milk	60g	1/4 cup
Unsalted butter, melted and slightly cooled	56g	4 tablespoons
Eggs	100g	2 large
Vanilla extract	—	2 teaspoons
Brown sugar	100g	1/2 cup
Fine sea salt	8g	3/4 teaspoon
Bread flour	325g	2 1/2 cups, spooned and leveled
Whole wheat or white whole wheat flour	70g	1/2 cup, spooned and leveled
Ground ginger	—	1 1/2 teaspoons
Ground cinnamon	—	1 teaspoon
Ground cloves	—	Pinch
Instant yeast	—	2 teaspoons
Chopped candied ginger (optional)	40g	1/4 cup

continued →

Gingery Apple Cake
continued

Make the topping: In a small bowl, combine the granulated sugar, butter, and salt and use your fingers to mix them together until moist crumbles form. Store in the refrigerator until it's time to use.

To bake in a bread machine: In the order listed, add all the cake ingredients (except for the candied ginger) to the bread machine's baking pan. Program the machine to its QUICK or RAPID WHITE setting and MEDIUM crust. Lock the pan into the machine, close the lid, and press START. When the alert for additions sounds, add the candied ginger, if using. Near the time that your dough begins its final rise (usually about 1:30 from completion), open your machine and scatter the topping evenly over the top of the loaf. Once the baking cycle is complete, remove the bread from the machine and tip the loaf out of the pan onto a cooling rack and cool for at least 15 minutes before slicing.

To bake in a home oven: In the order listed, add all the cake ingredients (except for the candied ginger) to the bread machine's baking pan. Select DOUGH, lock the pan into the machine, close the lid, and press START. When the alert for additions sounds, add the candied ginger, if using. At the completion of the cycle, the dough should be doubled in size; if not, leave it in the machine for additional time as needed.

Transfer the dough to a well-buttered 8- or 9-inch cake pan, using greased hands to gently stretch and shape it to fill the pan, without deflating it too much (it will be a wet dough). Cover loosely with food wrap and allow to proof until doubled in size, 45 to 60 minutes.

Meanwhile, preheat the oven to 350°F.

Sprinkle the topping over the proofed dough. Transfer to the oven and bake until domed and set in the center, 35 to 45 minutes.

Cool for at least 15 minutes in the pan before slicing and serving.

Leftovers and Storage: Best on the day it's made. Revive leftovers by wrapping in foil and rewarming in a 300°F oven for 10 to 15 minutes. Stored in an airtight bag or container, the sliced cake can be frozen for up to 1 month.

Matcha Ricotta Tea Cake

The color of this cake is just as striking as its flavor, thanks to the unmistakable presence of matcha. It's a lightly sweet loaf with just enough richness from whole-milk ricotta that it can be served plain as a light afternoon sweet, or as a base for fresh or stewed fruit and cream in an after-dinner dessert. Be sure to use pure matcha powder, not a green tea blend that contains only trace amounts of it.

Makes 1 loaf cake

Ingredient	Grams	Volume
Whole milk	120g	1/2 cup
Whole milk ricotta	120g	1/2 cup
Eggs	100g	2 large
Vanilla extract	8g	2 teaspoons
Sugar	110g	1/2 cup
Unsalted butter, cut into cubes, at room temperature	42g	3 tablespoons
Fine sea salt	8g	3/4 teaspoon
Bread flour	440g	3 cups plus 6 tablespoons, spooned and leveled
Matcha powder	14g	2 tablespoons
Instant yeast	—	2 teaspoons
Egg white or other crust-browning wash (optional; see page 26)	—	—

continued →

Matcha Ricotta Tea Cake
continued

To bake in a bread machine: In the order listed, add all the ingredients (except for the egg white) to the bread machine's baking pan. Program the machine to its **WHITE** setting and **MEDIUM** crust. Lock the pan into the machine, close the lid, and press **START**. If desired, after the loaf's final rise (usually around 1:30 from completion), pause the program and brush the proofed loaf with egg white. Once complete, remove the bread from the machine and let cool in the pan for 10 to 15 minutes. Then tip the loaf out of the pan onto a cooling rack to cool completely before slicing.

To bake in a home oven: In the order listed, add all the ingredients (except for the egg white) to the bread machine's baking pan. Select **DOUGH**, lock the pan into the machine, close the lid, and press **START**. At the completion of the cycle, the dough should be doubled in size; if not, leave it in the machine for additional time as needed.

Transfer the dough to a clean work surface. If it's too sticky to handle, dust it lightly with flour, but resist adding any more than necessary, and use a bench scraper to help lift and move it around. Gently stretch it to a thickness of about 1 inch, then shape to fit a 9 × 5-inch loaf pan (see page 30, for tips).

Place it seam-side down in a greased loaf pan. Cover with a clean towel or food wrap and proof in a warm spot in the kitchen until doubled in size, about 1 hour. You can also proof the dough overnight in the refrigerator; allow it to warm up at room temperature for 30 to 60 minutes before baking.

Preheat the oven to 350°F, using convection if available.

If desired, brush the top of the bread with egg white. Bake until browned and hollow-sounding when you tap on the loaf or an instant-read thermometer reads 190°F, 40 to 50 minutes.

Cool in the pan for at least 15 minutes. Then tip out onto a cooling rack to cool completely before slicing.

Leftovers and Storage: Best on the day it's made. Revive leftovers by wrapping in foil and rewarming in a 300°F oven for 10 to 15 minutes, or use them for French Toast (page 198). Stored in an airtight bag or container, the sliced cake can be frozen for up to 1 month.

Tender Almond Cake

This hands-off cake showcases both the alluring perfume of almonds, and their unique tenderness. It manages to be equally light and rich, and just tangy enough to invite a second bite. As with all the cakes in this chapter, this is lighter than its more familiar pound cake counterpart, so feel free to dress it up with fresh fruit and whipped cream (or yogurt or crème fraîche), or serve it plain with coffee or tea.

Makes 1 loaf cake

Ingredient	Grams	Volume
Cake		
Sour cream	120g	1/2 cup
Whole milk	120g	1/2 cup
Eggs	100g	2 large
Almond extract	—	1 tablespoon
Sugar	110g	1/2 cup
Unsalted butter, melted	56g	4 tablespoons
Fine sea salt	8g	3/4 teaspoon
Bread flour	357g	2 3/4 cups, spooned and leveled
Almond flour	100g	1 cup, spooned and leveled
Instant yeast	—	2 teaspoons
Topping		
Sliced almonds	20g	1/4 cup
Sugar	13g	2 tablespoons

continued →

Tender Almond Cake
continued

To bake in a bread machine: In the order listed, add all the cake ingredients to the bread machine's baking pan. Program the machine to its **QUICK** or **RAPID WHITE** setting and **MEDIUM** crust. Lock the pan into the machine, close the lid, and press **START**. Near the time that your dough begins its final rise (usually about 1:30 from completion), open your machine and scatter the topping of sliced almonds and sugar evenly over the loaf. Once the baking cycle is complete, remove the bread from the machine and tip the loaf out of the pan onto a cooling rack and cool for at least 15 minutes before slicing.

To bake in a home oven: In the order listed, add all the cake ingredients to the bread machine's baking pan. Select **DOUGH**, lock the pan into the machine, close the lid, and press **START**. At the completion of the cycle, the dough should be doubled in size; if not, leave it in the machine for additional time as needed.

Transfer the dough to a well-buttered 8- or 9-inch cake pan, using greased hands to gently stretch and shape it to fill the pan, without deflating it too much (it will be a wet dough). Cover loosely with food wrap and allow to proof until doubled in size, 45 to 60 minutes. Meanwhile, preheat the oven to 350°F.

Sprinkle the sliced almonds and topping sugar over the proofed dough. Transfer to the oven and bake until domed and set in the center, 35 to 45 minutes.

Cool for at least 15 minutes in the pan before slicing and serving.

Leftovers and Storage: Best on the day it's made. Revive leftovers by wrapping in foil and rewarming in a 300°F oven for 10 to 15 minutes, or use them for French Toast (page 198). Stored in an airtight bag or container, the sliced cake can be frozen for up to 1 month.

Variation

Hazelnut Cake: Substitute hazelnut flour/meal for the almond flour, vanilla extract for almond, and use finely chopped hazelnuts in the topping instead of sliced almonds.

A Few Simple Recipes for Leftover Bread

Bread Crumbs

Bread crumbs are valuable to have around for binding and breading needs, but also an easy and elevating garnish for salads, soups, and pasta when they're toasted with olive oil until crispy.

MAKES ABOUT 2 CUPS

6 cups (300g) cubed or torn bread

Extra-virgin olive oil (optional)

Fine sea salt (optional)

Put the bread in a food processor and pulse until coarsely ground. Spread the crumbs out on a sheet pan and allow to fully dry out overnight in a draft-free spot, or in the oven with just the pilot light on. Transfer to an airtight container and keep in the freezer for up to 3 months.

To use the bread crumbs as a garnish or topping, for every 1 cup bread crumbs, mix with 1 tablespoon extra-virgin olive oil, and toast in a skillet over medium-low heat, stirring often, until golden-brown and crisp. Season with salt to taste.

Craggy Skillet Croutons

These made-to-order croutons are ideal for soups and salads—they retain some of the chewy freshness of the good bread.

MAKES ABOUT 2 CUPS

2 cups (100g) coarsely torn day-old bread

About 3 tablespoons extra-virgin olive oil or butter

Fine sea salt

Set a heavy skillet over medium-low heat and allow it to preheat. When it's hot, cover the bottom with a thin film of olive oil or butter. Add the bread and gently toast, turning and stirring frequently, adjusting the heat to maintain a gentle sizzle, until golden brown and toasted all over.

Croque Fill-in-the-Blank

An iconic fork-and-knife sandwich, this is best made with a soft, plush sandwich bread. Ham is the classic filling, but it's a terrific vessel for roasted vegetables, too.

MAKES UP TO 4 SANDWICHES

FOR 1 CUP BÉCHAMEL

2 tablespoons unsalted butter

1½ tablespoons all-purpose flour

1 cup whole milk

Fine sea salt

Freshly ground black pepper

Freshly grated nutmeg (optional)

FOR EACH SANDWICH

3 to 4 tablespoons béchamel

2 slices sandwich bread

A few slices Gruyère or other nicely melting cheese

A few slices ham, or about ½ cup roasted mushrooms, squash, or broccoli; or sauteed hearty greens

1 fried egg (optional)

Make the béchamel: Melt the butter over medium heat in a small saucepan, and then whisk in the flour. Cook for a minute or two until the mixture smells very lightly toasted, then gradually whisk in the milk. Bring to a simmer (not a boil) and cook, stirring often, until thickened, 5 to 8 minutes. Season with salt, pepper, and a few pinches of nutmeg if desired.

Preheat the oven to 350°F. Line a baking sheet with parchment paper.

For each sandwich, spread a heaping tablespoon of béchamel on two slices of bread, then cover one side with cheese and your fillings of choice and close it up.

Arrange the assembled sandwich(es) on the baking sheet and spread the tops with an additional 1 to 2 tablespoons béchamel. Bake until the béchamel is slightly blistered and the fillings are melty and oozy. Top with a fried egg if you please.

Bread Pudding

Keep your leftover sweet or enriched breads in a bag in the freezer, and when it fills up, you can whip up a batch of this richly satisfying dessert, made from the humblest of leftovers.

MAKES 6 SERVINGS

2 tablespoons unsalted butter, melted, plus softened butter for greasing

6 cups (300g) cubed or torn day-old bread

2 cups whole milk

3 large eggs

¼ cup sugar

1 tablespoon honey

1 tablespoon whiskey or bourbon

¼ teaspoon fine sea salt

Preheat the oven to 350°F. Grease a 2-quart baking dish with softened butter.

Spread the bread out in the baking dish. In a bowl or large measuring glass, whisk together the milk, eggs, sugar, melted butter, honey, whiskey or bourbon, and salt until combined. Pour the mixture over the bread and press gently on the surface, to encourage the bread to soak up the custard. Allow to sit for about 1 hour.

Bake until just set in the center and the top is lightly browned, 35 to 45 minutes. Serve hot or warm, perhaps with a scoop of ice cream.

Overnight Breakfast Strata

My family's Christmas mornings always include a cheesy, "breakfast casserole" like this one, that's assembled the night prior. Soft, savory or sourdough breads work best.

MAKES 8 SERVINGS

Softened butter, for greasing

6 cups (300g) cubed or torn day-old bread

1½ cups coarsely shredded cheddar, plus more for sprinkling

1½ cups fillings of choice: browned sausage, crumbled bacon, roasted mushrooms, caramelized onions, cubes of roasted squash, wilted (and squeezed dry) greens

6 eggs

1¼ cups whole milk

1 tablespoon Dijon mustard

½ teaspoon fine sea salt

Freshly ground black pepper

Preheat the oven to 350°F. Grease a 2-quart baking dish with butter.

In the baking dish, use your hands to combine the bread, cheese, and fillings. In a tall pitcher or bowl whisk together the eggs, milk, Dijon, salt, and several grinds of black pepper. Pour the mixture over the bread, and gently press on the surface so that all the bread is moistened. Sprinkle with additional cheese. Let sit for at least 1 hour at room temperature, or covered with foil, overnight in the refrigerator.

Cover the pan with foil and bake for 30 minutes. Remove the foil and continue baking until browned and set in the center, 20 to 30 minutes more. Serve warm.

Simple French Toast

The smell of French toast sizzling in butter can make anybody a morning person. And sprinkling sugar over the slices as they fry creates the most delicious crust, a technique I learned from Julia Moskin in the New York Times.

MAKES 4 SERVINGS

2 eggs

1⅓ cups whole milk

Pinch fine sea salt

1 teaspoon vanilla extract or bourbon (optional)

4 thick slices fresh or day-old bread

Butter, for frying

About ¼ cup granulated sugar

In a wide, shallow bowl or baking dish, whisk together the eggs, milk, salt, and vanilla, if using.

Set a skillet over medium heat and allow to preheat thoroughly. Once hot, add a pat of butter and swirl it to evenly coat the pan.

Dip the bread in the custard mixture, flipping it once and allowing it to briefly absorb the liquid, then add to the hot pan. Repeat with as many slices of bread as will fit in an even layer. Sprinkle the tops of each slice evenly with about ½ tablespoon of sugar while the bottom cooks. Once it's golden brown, after 2 to 3 minutes, flip it over to cook the opposite side until browned, and sprinkle the exposed top with sugar. Flip once more, cooking just to melt the sugar, then remove from the heat.

Spread the cooked French toast out on a baking sheet and keep warm in a 275°F oven, until you're ready to serve.

Pressed Greens & Cheese

This sandwich is equal parts vegetables and cheese, and adding a weight as it sears helps to achieve a brilliantly buttery, crispy exterior.

MAKES 4 SANDWICHES

About 1 cup wilted and squeezed-dry greens (kale, Swiss chard, broccoli rabe, spinach)

3 tablespoons minced shallot or red onion

2 tablespoons coarsely chopped pickled chilies or Calabrian chilies (optional)

1 tablespoon red wine vinegar

About 1 cup (packed) grated cheddar, mozzarella, or provolone cheese

8 slices sandwich bread

Mayonnaise (optional)

Butter, for griddling

In a mixing bowl, combine the greens with the shallot, chilies, vinegar, and grated cheese.

For each sandwich, spread 2 pieces of bread with mayonnaise, and fill with about 1/2 cup of the greens-and-cheese mixture, spreading it evenly over the bread. Close them up.

Set a heavy skillet over medium-low heat. While it preheats, fleck butter over the top of the sandwiches, then add them to the hot pan buttered-side down, as many as will fit comfortably in an even layer. Pressing with a spatula or setting another skillet on top, weigh down the sandwiches as they sear. Cook until golden-brown and crisp, 3 to 6 minutes. Fleck butter over the tops, flip them over, and repeat to sear the opposite sides. Serve hot.

Wheat-y Sourdough Discard Pancakes

Collecting sourdough discard during the week is a pleasure with these pancakes as a weekend reward. They're fluffy but fortifying, and best using discard that's less than a week old.

MAKES 10 TO 12 PANCAKES

1 cup (140g) whole-wheat flour

2 teaspoons baking powder

1/2 teaspoon fine sea salt

1 cup (240g) plain yogurt or buttermilk

2 eggs

2 tablespoons avocado oil or melted coconut oil, plus more for frying

2 tablespoons maple syrup

1 teaspoon vanilla extract

1 cup (100g) sourdough discard, ideally less than a week old (page 129)

In one bowl, whisk together the flour, baking powder, and salt. In another one or a tall pitcher, combine the yogurt, eggs, oil, maple syrup, and vanilla extract, then whisk in the sourdough discard. Fold the wet ingredients into the dry until just combined.

Set a nonstick skillet over medium heat and allow to preheat thoroughly. Brush with a small amount of avocado or coconut oil, then fry pancakes in dollops of 2 to 3 tablespoons each, spreading them out a bit to flatten them, until bubbles appear on the surface, about 2 minutes. Then flip and continue cooking until set in the centers, another 1 to 2 minutes.

Spread cooked pancakes out on a baking sheet and keep warm in a 275°F oven, until you're ready to serve.

Weight Conversions

Ingredient	Gram weight	Volume
Flours & Grains		
all-purpose flour	130 grams	1 cup
barley flour	120 grams	1 cup
bread flour	130 grams	1 cup
buckwheat flour	140 grams	1 cup
cornmeal, fine-grind	150 grams	1 cup
einkorn flour	130 grams	1 cup
gluten-free flour blend	135 grams	1 cup
oat flour	120 grams	1 cup
oats, instant	120 grams	1 cup
rye flour	140 grams	1 cup
spelt flour	140 grams	1 cup
whole wheat flour	140 grams	1 cup
Dry Sugars & Seasonings		
brown sugar	220 grams	1 cup, packed
cinnamon, ground	8 grams	1 tablespoon
cocoa powder	70 grams	1 cup
coconut sugar	11 grams	1 tablespoon
granulated sugar	220 grams	1 cup
fine sea salt	7 grams	1 teaspoon

Ingredient	Gram weight	Volume
Liquids & Fats		
avocado oil	11 grams	1 tablespoon
butter	14 grams	1 tablespoon
honey	20 grams	1 tablespoon
maple syrup	21 grams	1 tablespoon
molasses	21 grams	1 tablespoon
olive oil	11 grams	1 tablespoon
tahini	15 grams	1 tablespoon
water	240 grams	1 cup
yogurt, plain	240 grams	1 cup
Nuts & Seeds		
flaxseeds	11 grams	1 tablespoon
pecans	100 grams	1 cup
sesame seeds	10 grams	1 tablespoon
sunflower seeds, hulled	160 grams	1 cup
walnuts	100 grams	1 cup

Acknowledgments

At Ten Speed Press, thank you Molly Birnbaum for giving me the opportunity (and a great deal of latitude) to write this book, and Cristina Garces for your expert editorial steering. Thank you Annie Marino for your collaborative approach with regard to photography and design, and the entire Ten Speed Press team for being such an incredibly kind and high-functioning operation: Natalie Blachere, Jane Chinn, Kate Slate, Rachel Holzman, Lauren Chung, Ken DellaPenta, and Allison Renzulli.

Thank you Alison Fargis of Stonesong Literary for your advocacy and friendship, and the whole Stonesong family.

The photoshoot for this book was a joyful dream for me. Immense, heartfelt thanks Trevor Baca (photographer) and Paul Wang (kitchen genius) for your incredible talents and friendship. It's not often that I finish up a big, exhausting project and feel like I could immediately do it all over again, but being part of such a fun, creative, hardworking, lean team with you two had that effect. Thank you, Ed Gallagher, for your artist eye and no-stress energy in pulling together all the beautiful props.

Thanks to recipe testers Jordan Smith, Paul Wang, Max Volger, and my nieces Ali and Zoe Volger. And thanks to the many friends and neighbors who allowed me to offload my bread surplus over the course of writing this book, particularly the trainers at Brooklyn Athletic Club.

Thank you King Arthur Baking Co., Hayden Flour Mills, Barton Spring Mills, and Maine Grains for sharing your top-tier flours with me, and for being such wonderful, nurturing businesses and collaborators that I continually learn and benefit from. Thank you Cuisinart and Zojirushi for providing bread machines to use in our photoshoot, as well as Material Kitchen for sharing a few of your elegant serrated knives.

And thank you as always to my parents and my family, in this instance for granting me reins to the bread machine way back in the '90s, and broadly for your unflagging support. Thank you Vincent Abrams for bearing with me through all of this bread, and for the gift of your love and partnership.

Index

Published in the United States by Ten Speed Press, an imprint of the Crown Publishing Group, a division of Penguin Random House LLC, New York.
TenSpeed.com

Ten Speed Press and the Ten Speed Press colophon are registered trademarks of Penguin Random House LLC.

Typefaces: Colophon Foundry's Grenette and 205TF's Muoto

Library of Congress Cataloging-in-Publication Data
Names: Volger, Lukas, author. | Baca, Trevor (Photographer), photographer. Title: The bread machine book : 75 unforgettable, unfussy recipes for every baker / Lukas Volger ; photographs by Trevor Baca. Identifiers: LCCN 2024012363 (print) | LCCN 2024012364 (ebook) | ISBN 9780593835432 (hardcover) | ISBN 9780593835449 (ebook) Subjects: LCSH: Cooking (Bread) | Bread. | LCGFT: Cookbooks. Classification: LCC TX769 .V64 2025 (print) | LCC TX769 (ebook) | DDC 641.81/5—dc23/eng/20240328
LC record available at https://lccn.loc.gov/2024012363
LC ebook record available at https://lccn.loc.gov/2024012364

Hardcover ISBN: 978-0-593-83543-2
eBook ISBN: 978-0-593-83544-9

Printed in China

Editor: Cristina Garces | Production editor: Natalie Blachere
Designer and art director: Annie Marino | Production designers: Mari Gill and Faith Hague
Production manager: Jane Chinn | Prepress color manager: Claudia Sanchez
Kitchen manager: Paul Wang
Copyeditor: Kate Slate | Proofreader: Rachel Holzman | Indexer: Ken DellaPenta
Publicist: Lauren Chung | Marketer: Allison Renzulli

10 9 8 7 6 5 4 3 2 1

First Edition